M000214381

WHY

Answering Life's
Most Important Question

JESUS?

RAY COMFORT

BroadStreet
PUBLISHING

BroadStreet Publishing® Group, LLC
Savage, Minnesota, USA
BroadStreetPublishing.com

Why Jesus?: Answering Life's Most Important Question
Copyright © 2023 Ray Comfort

9781424566105 (faux leather)
9781424566112 (ebook)

All video and email transcripts have been lightly edited for readability and clarity.

Stock or custom editions of BroadStreet Publishing titles may be purchased in bulk for educational, business, ministry, fundraising, or sales promotional use. For information, please email orders@broadstreetpublishing.com.

Cover and interior by Garborg Design Works | garborgdesign.com

Printed in China

23 24 25 26 27 5 4 3 2 1

To my faithful cameraman and friend,
Yale Chiang.

CONTENTS

INTRODUCTION

This book was a first. I have never deconstructed and explained witnessing encounters in written form before, and I loved every minute. But I had one hesitation.

There was a time when teaching someone to drive wasn't easy. Those were the days of the dreaded stick shift, when, to change gears, you had to have the right timing of clutch-in and clutch-out. If you didn't get it right, it was very embarrassing—with a terrible grating sound and a jerky vehicle that lunged forward uncontrollably. But nowadays, driving a car with automatic gears is so easy a child can do it. Take for instance the eight-year-old boy who craved a cheeseburger, hopped into his father's car, and drove himself and his younger sister to a McDonald's near their Ohio home:

> Police arrived at the McDonald's in East Palestine, Ohio, around 8 p.m. Sunday after receiving multiple calls from people who saw the young boy driving, the *Weirton Daily Times* reported. According to authorities, the children headed to McDonald's after their parents fell asleep early. During the mile and a half road trip, the 8-year-old obeyed all traffic laws and drove "effortlessly" through downtown, East Palestine Patrolman Jacob Koehler told the *Times*. "He

didn't hit a single thing on the way there. It was unreal," he said. The 8-year-old used money from his piggy bank to pay for the food.[1]

Driving a car is simple. You get in, turn it on, put it in drive, push the accelerator, and steer it in the direction you desire. But there are a few extra things we would want to say to a new driver:

1. You are driving a weapon that has the potential to kill other human beings.
2. You must stay on the right side of the road.
3. Stay sober.
4. Don't text while driving.
5. Obey the speed limit.
6. Continually be on the alert for road signs.
7. Keep a close eye on those who are in adjacent lanes, behind you, and in front of you.
8. If the person in the car you are following suddenly slams on his or her brakes and you plow into it causing injuries, you could find yourself facing a serious lawsuit.
9. Be ready for parked motorists who thoughtlessly open the driver's door without looking to see if you're approaching. You should also watch for dogs, cats, and kids who might run out from between parked cars.

10. Plus, there are cyclists you pass who could easily end up crushed under your wheel if you don't give them a wide berth.

All these dos and don'ts could turn you against ever wanting to experience the joy and convenience of driving. And that was my hesitation in writing this book. I want you to experience the joy of sharing the gospel with the lost, but as I analyze each witnessing encounter, I don't want you to be discouraged by what *sounds* complex. Much is going on, but in reality (like driving), it is a simple process that just entails common sense and a learned skill, which will, in time, take place without a second thought. The gears will change automatically.

In the following chapters, you'll see me use very similar gospel presentations with different people. While some find this tedious, others are trained by the repetition until their gears shift without effort. Seeing how people react to hearing the gospel gives them the confidence to go through the Ten Commandments with those around them, even using the analogies they have seen work. They help the lost understand their state before God. The following is an encouraging email I received from a woman who did just this:

Dear Ray,

Somewhere in the world just now, a young man is either saved or at least reading his bedside, yet-untouched Bible. Praise the Lord!

I pulled what we're calling a "total Ray" on him. To my surprise, he'd never heard the gospel. Shocking, huh! When he heard the parachute-versus-flapping-arms part, he was completely attentive and said, "Wow, I've never heard it put like that before, but it makes total sense. No one would refuse the parachute!" Actually, witnessing was easy considering we were a few miles up. I figured what's better than being on a plane to make someone think of dying, right?

What started as a clerical error—that is, our seats got separated—turned out for someone's potential salvation. He said he'd go back to reading his neglected Bible and would never see anything the same way again. Brilliant! And don't worry. I'm completely unafraid of using the word *hell*. So if we see him in glory, we'll know the Holy Spirit scared him enough. Thank God for your YouTube videos. Bless you, precious brother!

Much love in Jesus,
Deb

You don't have to be the bravest or be the most eloquent or have all the answers to share the gospel. What I've learned in my many years of witnessing is that every encounter, every conversation, every time I use the law to expose someone's sin is all about revealing the answer to one question: Why Jesus? And this question expands into many: Why did Jesus suffer and die on the cross? Why did Jesus rise from the dead? Why is Jesus the *only* way to salvation and eternal life? The answer is the gospel. The answer is what changes people's lives.

May God use this book to take you to new and great places.

Ray Comfort

CHAPTER 1

GOOD PEOPLE

When I first filmed a witnessing encounter way back in the late 1990s, I never dreamed for a moment that years later, those videos would end up on something called "YouTube" on "the internet," let alone that they would get more than two hundred million views.

That first video was called "Seal Beach Kid," and in it, I showed a very polite young man why he needed Jesus. More than two decades later, I still explain the same simple gospel—summed up in one question: "Why Jesus?"

Getting people to come on camera isn't easy. Most respond to my "Would you like to be on YouTube?" with a quick but firm "No, thank you." If they ask what it's about, I respond, "I ask people if they think there's an afterlife. What do you think?" When they give their thoughts, I say, "That's interesting. Will you give me five minutes for an interview?" If they say they will, I turn my camera on, point it at them, and ask, "May I have permission to interview you for YouTube and for all media purposes?" They say yes, and away we go.

In the following transcript, you'll see conversations I had with Abram and Elena. We recorded these on different days, but we've merged them together so that you can see two different people who both believe they're good encounter the same gospel message. Abram surprised me with what he said, and Elena was a friendly woman.

RAY: If you died today, where would you go?

ABRAM: I say hell because everyone is not perfect, but Jesus died for our sins on the cross. So, he paid the price for us to have eternal life.

RAY: So why aren't you going to heaven then if that's true?

ABRAM: I have to repent and give my life to Jesus.

RAY: So that hasn't happened yet?

ABRAM: I'm working on it.

RAY: You're working on it. Let's see if we can speed up that process. [TO ELENA] The promise of the Bible is for everlasting life. In the Old Testament, God says, "I'm going to destroy death for you" [see Isaiah 25:8]. The New

Testament tells us how he did it. Can you think of a way to prove the Bible's the Word of God? Because there is a way. The Bible says in the book of Acts that the apostle Paul used [Bible prophecy] when he reasoned with people about Jesus. He did so out of the law of Moses and out of the prophets. He used prophecy. Prophecy for the Messiah.

But we've gotten prophecy for the last two thousand years. Jesus said, way back two thousand years ago, that the Jews would get Jerusalem back. That's one undeniable prophecy we've seen fulfilled in 1967 after two thousand years without a homeland. God said, "I'll scatter you throughout the whole earth, and I'll draw you back to Jerusalem, to Israel" [author's paraphrase; see Isaiah 11:11–12; Jeremiah 31]. That happened in 1967 [Israel became a nation in 1949 but didn't possess Jerusalem until 1967], and that shows us that God knows the future. If he knows the future, he's the Creator of the universe, and the Bible's the Word of God—and its promise of everlasting life is true. Do you think it's okay for a Christian to use bad language?

ELENA: No.

RAY: I heard you use a bad word.

ELENA: I know. I'm quick to lose my temper sometimes.

RAY: You weren't losing your temper. You were just talking.

ELENA: It was because me and my boyfriend… we've had a rough morning already.

RAY: I'm going to be very personal with you. Are you having sex with your boyfriend?

ELENA: Uh, yes.

RAY: What do you think God thinks of that?

ELENA: He probably doesn't think that it's the best thing.

RAY: Remember, the Scriptures say, "Fornicators will not inherit the kingdom of God" [1 Corinthians 6:9–10, author's paraphrase]. Elena, I want to see you in heaven, so I'm going to give you a little test. Do you think you're a good person?

ELENA: Yes.

I asked this question based on what Jesus did: "Now as He was going out on the road, one came running, knelt before Him, and asked Him, 'Good Teacher, what shall I do that I may inherit eternal life?' So Jesus said to him, 'Why do you call Me good? No one is good but One, that is, God'" (Mark 10:17–18).

Arguably, the number one reason most people don't see the need for the Savior is that they think they are morally good. This is based on their lack of understanding of God's righteousness. Elena had a similar response. And so did Abram.

> RAY [TO ABRAM]: How many lies have you told in your life?
>
> ABRAM: A lot.
>
> RAY: A lot? So, what do you call someone who tells lies?
>
> ABRAM: A bad person.
>
> RAY: No, they're called a liar.

Perhaps you are cringing a little as I speak such strong words to Abram and Elena. So, let me address that concern by saying that I am *very* careful to watch my tone. I deliberately cultivate a good bedside manner, never speaking with a harsh tone although my words are serious. A doctor often *needs* to say heavy things to his patient. Perhaps the doctor tells the patient that he is overweight and needs to change his lifestyle or his diet will kill him. The doctor can either say these things with a harsh tone or cultivate his words with a genuine concern. That's what I strive to do. Please know that my words issue from a deep concern for these people. If they are not awakened to their terrible danger, they won't flee from God's wrath. Think of the tone you would have for someone who remains in bed in a burning house. It would be mingled with love, a deep concern, and a tremendous urgency.

Also, keep in mind that not all gifts are material. We can give someone love. We can give them joy. What I'm seeking to do is give an immaterial gift that this world wouldn't even consider a gift. They would consider it a curse rather than a blessing. But it certainly is a gift—one that leads to something infinitely greater. I am wanting to instill "the beginning of wisdom" (Proverbs 9:10), to cause someone to truly fear God. I want them to tremble at the very thought of offending him because, hopefully, this will lead to a godly sorrow, which produces repentance, which leads to eternal life.

When the Corinthians were given to sin, the apostle Paul gave them some very strong rebukes. But then he said, "For even if I made you sorry with my letter, I do not regret it; though I did regret it. For I perceive that the same epistle made you sorry, though only for a while. Now I rejoice, not that you were made sorry, but that your sorrow led to repentance. For you were made sorry in a godly manner, that you might suffer loss from us in nothing. For godly sorrow produces repentance leading to salvation, not to be regretted; but the sorrow of the world produces death" (2 Corinthians 7:8–10).

While the world may not always see the purpose of our words, this shouldn't stop us from speaking. Proverbs 28:23 says, "He who rebukes a man will find more favor afterward than he who flatters with the tongue." I speak with a gentle tone so that my listeners will understand that my goal is to show them the hope found only in Jesus, not to criticize or judge them.

> RAY: Now, do you still think you're a good person?
>
> ABRAM: Not really.
>
> RAY: When did you last look at a woman with lust? Because Jesus said when...
>
> ABRAM: Everyone has. Everyone has because, like, everyone's not perfect.
>
> RAY: Jesus said, "Whoever looks at a woman to lust for her has already committed adultery with her in his heart" [Matthew 5:28]. Did you know that?
>
> ABRAM: Yes.
>
> RAY: So, you've looked at women with lust?
>
> ABRAM: Yes.
>
> RAY: Have you ever stolen something in your life?
>
> ABRAM: I've not stolen.
>
> RAY: Never stolen.

ABRAM: Maybe stolen a pencil but not something that serious.

RAY: The value of that which you steal is irrelevant. If you open my wallet and just take out one dollar, you're guilty of theft as much as if you took out a hundred dollars.

ABRAM: Yes.

RAY: So, that which you steal is irrelevant. God doesn't say, "Oh, he's stolen, but it's not of value, so he's not a thief." No, if you steal one thing, you're a thief in God's eyes. So, we're trying to get rid of your self-righteousness. Do you know what self-righteousness is?

ABRAM: No.

RAY: It's someone who thinks they're a good person when they're not; and none of us are good.

RAY [TO ELENA]: Have you ever used God's name in vain?

ELENA: I try not to.

RAY: OMG?

ELENA: So yes, I may have sinned. Yes, I may have lied. Yes, I may have, you know, taken the Lord's name in vain or fornicated with my boyfriend, but that doesn't make me not a good person.

Can you see the battle going on here? Elena trusted in the conviction that she was a good person. She was clinging to a parachute that was filled with holes and refused to let it go. I needed to convince her that she wasn't the good person she believed she was. She, therefore, needed more of God's law. Same with Abram.

RAY: Have you ever used God's name in vain?

ABRAM: Oh yes.

RAY: Would you use your mother's name as a cuss word.

ABRAM: No.

RAY: Instead of using [a swear word], you'd use her name in its place?

ABRAM: No.

RAY: Now tell me, why wouldn't you do that?

ABRAM: Because she's my mom.

Analogies can be so powerful in that they can show the lost another perspective. Mine aren't copyrighted. Please use them if you think they can help your witness.

RAY: What does that mean…you respect her?

ABRAM: Yes.

RAY: But you don't respect God. The Bible says his name is holy, and you've used his name in place of that [swear] word to express disgust. Abram, that's so serious it's called blasphemy, punishable by death in the Old Testament. Have you ever hated somebody?

ABRAM: Yes, I would say that.

RAY: The Bible says, "He who hates his brother is a murderer" [1 John 3:15, author's paraphrase]. So, I'm just going to give you a quick summation of this little court case. This is for you to judge yourself. I'm not judging you. You've told me you're a lying, thieving, blasphemous adulterer at heart, and you have to face God on judgment day. If he judges you by the Ten Commandments (we've looked at four), are you going to be innocent or guilty?

ABRAM: I'll be guilty.

RAY: Heaven or hell?

ABRAM: Hell.

RAY: Now, does that concern you?

ABRAM: Yes.

RAY: So, what can you do to be saved? How can you be made right with God?

ABRAM: Repent.

RAY: And what else?

ABRAM: Follow his laws.

RAY: Well, you've forgotten something very important. Do you know what it is?

ABRAM: Believe that he died on the cross for us.

RAY: Repent and trust in Jesus. You've got to trust in him. [TO ELENA] It's very important to realize that there's such a thing as a false conversion, and Jesus warned that many on the day of judgment will say, "Lord, Lord, we did many wonderful things in your name" [Matthew 7:22, author's paraphrase]. He'll say, "Depart from me, you worker of lawlessness; I never knew you" [Matthew 7:23, author's paraphrase]. I don't want you to be in that category of people. I want you to...

ELENA: You want to warn Christians, right?

RAY: Yes, even the hypocrite, those who are sinning willfully and not bringing forth fruits that should accompany salvation. Now, tell me, what did God do for guilty sinners to save us from hell?

ELENA: He died on the cross.

RAY: I hope today you'll think about what Jesus did on the cross for you and that you'll make sure your heart is free from sin, and you won't willfully sin, and you'll have the things that accompany salvation. Where you spend eternity is so important, and I want to see you in heaven. Okay? So you're going to think about what we talked about?

ELENA: Yes, and I'm working on it. I could be upset about some of the things that you're asking me, or offended, or feel some type of way, but you know, what you're saying is the truth to remind me to walk like Christ.

My conversation with Elena left me encouraged. Now, let's turn back to Abram to see how he responded to the gospel message.

RAY [TO ABRAM]: Let me just give you a quick gospel presentation so you understand actually what happened on that cross. You and I broke God's law, the Ten Commandments, and Jesus paid the fine. Do you remember his last words? He said just before he dismissed his spirit…He said three very profound words, do you remember what they were? He said, "It is finished" [John 19:30]. He was saying that the debt's been paid. We broke God's law; Jesus paid the fine.

If you're in court, someone can pay your spending fines—and the judge will let you go even though you're guilty. God can let us go. He can let us live forever, forgive our sins, all because Jesus paid the fine in his life's blood. He can pardon us, grant us everlasting life as a free gift because Jesus suffered and died and rose again on the third day. And all you have to do to find everlasting life is repent and trust alone in Jesus. Don't trust your goodness; don't say, "I'm a good person," because you're not. Trust alone in Jesus. Is this making sense?

ABRAM: Yes, sir.

RAY: So, when are you going to repent and trust in Jesus?

ABRAM: Now.

RAY: Right now?

ABRAM: Yes, sir.

RAY: Can I pray with you?

ABRAM: You can.

RAY: Father, I pray for Abram. Thank you for his open, honest heart today. I pray he'll see his sin in its true light. In Jesus' name we pray, amen. Do you have a Bible at home?

ABRAM: Yes.

RAY: Can I give you a gift? [Hands Abram the Gospel of John]

ABRAM: Sure.

I almost always ask those to whom I share the gospel if they have a Bible, and even if they have one, I give them a copy of the Gospel of John. Some people ask if I then follow up and continue to disciple those I've spoken with. My answer is that I can't, and I shouldn't. As a married man, I can't ask young ladies for their contact information so that I can follow up with them. Instead, I commit people like Elena and Abram into the hands of a faithful Creator, knowing that he who has begun a good work in them will complete it if he so sees fit.

CHAPTER 2

MORE THAN JESUS LOVES YOU

If there's one thing that will hinder us in the task of evangelism, it's a fear of failure. But we should never fear failure because, more often than not, it is the avenue to success. And success for the Christian is faithfulness. It's not necessarily to reap a harvest. Rather, it's to faithfully plant the seed. Sometimes we get to reap, but more often we are sowing in tears (see Psalm 126:5). Sharing the gospel is often a depressing and thankless task, but our confidence is in the fact that God is faithful. It is his work.

Weep though we do at the hardness of some soil, God has given us his law to break up the ground. It is the plow we use to make way for the seed of the gospel. The commandments break up the hard soil of self-righteousness and prepare the heart for the grace of God in Christ because they are the best tool to reveal the sin that separates us from God. Therefore, our trust is in the Lord and in the tool he's provided. That makes this task much easier. Confidence in God is the shoehorn of evangelism. We often struggle to put on a shoe, but a shoehorn is designed to make it easier. Trusting in the Lord takes the struggle out of evangelism.

Anissa was perhaps in her twenties, innocent-looking, with a seemingly permanent smile on her face. The man with her was almost the opposite. He was very quiet, to the point of making me wonder if he was going to be contentious. I was wrong in that summation. He turned out to be very open.

RAY: Has anyone ever said to you, "Jesus loves you"?

ANISSA: Yes.

RAY: What did you think of that?

ANISSA: I thought it was nice that they told me that.

RAY: How do you know Jesus loves you?

ANISSA: Because my grandma told me before.

RAY [TO MAN]: Have you ever been told, "Jesus loves you"?

MAN: Yes.

RAY: What did you think…was it nice?

My use of the word *nice* is sanctified sarcasm. This is because our message to the world should be that they are in terrible danger. To tell them about the depths of our sin and the necessity of Jesus' crucifixion in a way that they conclude is "nice" is to betray our commission and do the ultimate disservice.

> MAN: Yes, it was nice.
>
> RAY: Anissa, did your grandma tell you anything else about the love of Christ? *Why* does Jesus love you, and how do you know he loves you?
>
> ANISSA: No, she never really got into details. She just told me that Jesus loves me.
>
> RAY: And that made you feel good?
>
> ANISSA: Yes.
>
> RAY: I'm going to show you *how much* Jesus loves you, but I'm going to do it in a very unusual way. Can you handle that? Can you be honest with me?

I make a habit of asking the person to whom I'm speaking if they can be honest with me. This is because the good-soil hearer in the parable of the sower is the one who has an honest and good heart. "But that on the good ground are they, which in an honest and good heart, having heard the word, keep it, and bring forth fruit with patience" (Luke 8:15 KJV).

In other words, they come clean about their sins. That was my hope with Anissa and the man with her.

> ANISSA: Yes, I think I can handle it.
>
> RAY: Do you think you're a good person?
>
> ANISSA: Yes.
>
> RAY [TO MAN]: What about you?
>
> MAN: I think I'm a good person.
>
> RAY: I'm going to challenge both of you on that. There's a reason for that. The Bible says, "Every man will proclaim his own goodness" [Proverbs 20:6, author's paraphrase]. We all think we're good people because we make the mistake of judging ourselves by our own moral standard, not by God's. Do you know what God's moral standard is?
>
> ANISSA: No.
>
> RAY [TO MAN]: Do you?
>
> MAN: Just follow the Ten Commandments?

It is common for sinners to think that they have kept the commandments. This is because they have never looked down the barrels of those ten great cannons. Our job is to bring sinners into the open, aim the cannons at them, and then, one by one, light each fuse.

While this may sound harsh, we are preparing sinners for what is to come on judgment day so that they take the opportunity they have now to turn from their sin and repent. It is the law that will judge them, so our hope is that they will see judgment as a fearful thing.

> For as many as have sinned without law will also perish without law, and as many as have sinned in the law will be judged by the law. (Romans 2:12)

> So speak and so do as those who will be judged by the law of liberty. (James 2:12)

How do we know that these Scriptures are speaking of the Ten Commandments when they say we will be judged by the law? Here is the context:

> You yourself are…an instructor of the foolish, a teacher of babes, having the form of knowledge and truth in the law. You, therefore, who teach another, do you not teach yourself? You who preach that a man should not steal, do you steal? You who say, "Do not commit adultery," do you commit adultery? You who abhor idols, do you rob temples? (Romans 2:19–22)

> For whoever shall keep the whole law, and yet stumble in one point, he is guilty of all. For He who said, "Do not commit adultery," also said,

"Do not murder." Now if you do not commit adultery, but you do murder, you have become a transgressor of the law. So speak and so do as those who will be judged by the law of liberty. (James 2:10–12)

Our understanding of the nature of God and of the terrible fate of the ungodly will dictate the passion with which we speak. The Bible says that it's a fearful thing to "fall into the hands of the living God" (Hebrews 10:31). If we "fall" into the hands of the enemy or if we "fall" into the hands of the law, the connotation is that we're in big trouble. And sinners are in big trouble with God. Death is just the first installment. It is evidence that God is angry at sinners. I would far rather fall onto the face of the sun than fall into the hands of the living God. That knowledge dictates my passion. But he isn't just angry at sinners. The Bible says his wrath abides on them (see John 3:36). Who would ever believe that about God? It's a very hard pill to swallow.

Yet all around us are God-created laws that show us the dangers of violating those laws. Fall just twenty feet onto concrete, and gravity will kill you. Merely touch a current of raw electricity for a few seconds, and it will almost certainly kill you. One lesson is to be careful when you climb and to stay away from raw electricity. An even greater lesson is that God's standard of morality is infinitely higher than ours. We may think we are good people, but in our hearts and by our actions, we have violated God's law. And if we violate the law of our holy, just Creator, it will kill us. The cold reality of our impending death should convince us that God is deadly serious about sin.

But thankfully, the law is also designed to dawn light on our sin, like the rising sun enlightens the early morning, which allows us to see our sin and repent before it's too late.

> RAY: Yes. How are you doing with the Ten Commandments? Are you following them? Are you breaking them? Keeping them?
>
> MAN: I feel like I'm doing all right.
>
> RAY [TO ANISSA]: Are you familiar with the Ten Commandments?
>
> ANISSA: Yes.
>
> RAY: Do you think you've kept them or broken them?
>
> ANISSA: For the most part, yes, I think I'm doing a pretty decent job. I'm not perfect, like he said.
>
> RAY: Which ones have you broken?
>
> ANISSA: Oh, let me think about it.

RAY: I can speed up your process. How many lies have you told in your life?

ANISSA: Probably a lot.

RAY: So that's the ninth. [TO MAN] Have you lied?

MAN: Yes.

RAY: So, you're a liar?

MAN: Yes.

Why *personalize* the sin? Because it is calling sinners out on their sin. It's not a fib, a mistake, or a white lie, and those who lie are liars. It is a turning of the mirror to the sinner and moving it close to his or her face. This will be of great benefit because "whoever *calls* on the name of the LORD shall be saved" (Acts 2:21, emphasis added). People won't *call* if they don't see their danger, and they won't see their danger if they don't see and own their sin.

RAY [TO ANISSA]: And what about you?

ANISSA: Yes.

RAY: You still think you're a good person?

ANISSA: Yes.

RAY: Have you ever stolen something in your whole life, even if it's small?

ANISSA: Yes.

RAY: What do you call someone who steals?

ANISSA: A stealer?

RAY: No, they're from Pittsburgh. A thief.

ANISSA: A thief.

RAY: So what are you?

ANISSA: A thief.

RAY: No, you're a lying thief. Do you still think you're a good person?

ANISSA: Yes.

Anissa was like a terminally ill patient who insisted that she was well. If she doesn't see her disease, she will never desire the cure. She needs to know that the law is wrathful. It's coming after her with terrible vengeance and will punish her for her sin. That thought is far from our mind if we think that we are morally good people. Look at what happened when God came in peace and gave his law to Israel:

> For you have not come to the mountain that
> may be touched and that burned with fire, and
> to blackness and darkness and tempest, and
> the sound of a trumpet and the voice of words,
> so that those who heard it begged that the
> word should not be spoken to them anymore.
> (For they could not endure what was com-
> manded: "And if so much as a beast touches

the mountain, it shall be stoned or shot with an arrow." And so terrifying was the sight that Moses said, "I am exceedingly afraid and trembling.") (Hebrews 12:18–21)

God wasn't expressing his wrath, and yet Moses trembled in fear. How much more will sinners tremble if they die in their sins and face him on what the Bible calls "the great and dreadful day of the LORD" (Malachi 4:5)?

RAY [TO MAN]: Have you stolen?

MAN: Yes.

RAY: You're a thief too?

MAN: Yes.

RAY: Do you think you're a good person?

MAN: Yes.

RAY [TO ANISSA]: Have you ever used God's name in vain?

ANISSA: Yes.

RAY: Would you use your mother's name as a cuss word?

ANISSA: No.

RAY: Tell me, why not?

ANISSA: She's done everything for me. She's, like, given up so much to have me in her life.

RAY: So, to use her name instead of [a cuss] word to express disgust would be a horrible thing to do, and yet you've done that with the name of the God who *gave* you your mother. That's called blasphemy. It's very, very serious. In fact, it's so serious, in God's eyes, it's punishable by death in the Old Testament. [TO MAN] Have you used God's name in vain?

MAN: By accident, yes.

RAY: "By accident." You didn't know what you're doing?

MAN: When I was a child, like four years old, yes.

RAY: You started blaspheming at four years old?

MAN: Yes.

The man was more than likely trying to trivialize his sin. His blasphemy was an accident. He was just a little child. It wasn't serious. I can't emphasize enough that my tone is never one of impatience and is always mingled with a genuine love and concern. While I was uncomfortable (and know that these two were also uncomfortable as they faced up to their sin), I could never let that hold me back from taking them through the law. Sin is deadly serious, and I knew that what I was doing was for their ultimate good.

RAY [TO ANISSA]: Okay, I appreciate your honesty. Jesus said that if you look with lust, you commit adultery in the heart [see Matthew 5:28]. Have you ever looked with lust?

ANISSA: No.

RAY [TO MAN]: Have you ever looked with lust?

MAN: Yes. It's more common with guys, so yes, I have looked with lust.

RAY: You have committed adultery in your heart. So, I'm going to give you a quick summation. I'm not judging you…I just met you guys. But you've told me that you're a lying, thieving, blasphemous adulterer at heart. [TO ANISSA] So you're a lying, thieving blasphemer. Here's the big question: If God judges you by the Ten Commandments on judgment day, do you think you'll be innocent or guilty?

ANISSA: I mean, I think Jesus or God is very understanding.

RAY: Do you know what you've just done?

ANISSA: What?

RAY: You've just broken the first and the second of the Ten Commandments. Do you know what they are? The second is "Don't make yourself a graven image," that's a false god. The first is

"Don't have any other gods before me" [Exodus 20:3–4, author's paraphrase]. Before I was a Christian, I broke those commandments. I had a god I felt comfortable with. A snugly, cuddly god, like a teddy bear, and if I sinned, it didn't really worry him. But the God of the Bible says, "The soul that sins, it shall die" [Ezekiel 18:20, author's paraphrase]. He says, "The wages of sin is death" [Romans 6:23]. So, if you are judged by the commandments on judgment day, are you going to be innocent or guilty?

ANISSA: Then, guilty.

RAY: Heaven or hell?

ANISSA: I don't know. Whatever God decides.

RAY: Well, the Bible says that all liars will have their part in the lake of fire—no thief, no blasphemer, no adulterer will inherit the kingdom of God [see Revelation 21:8; 1 Corinthians 6:9–10].

ANISSA: [Starts laughing]

RAY: So explain something to me. Why are you laughing?

ANISSA: Because I just saw my boss. [Her boss had just opened the door behind Ray.]

Despite possible interruptions, I never forget that there is a possibility that the person to whom I am speaking may not be alive tomorrow. That is a reality we need to keep in mind in case we lose a sense of urgency or we want to soften the message because we are uncomfortable. Listen to Charles Spurgeon resort to justified sarcasm to make this point:

> Ho, ho, sir surgeon, you are too delicate to tell the man that he is ill! You hope to heal the sick without their knowing it. You therefore flatter them; and what happens? They laugh at you; they dance upon their own graves. At last they die! Your delicacy is cruelty; your flatteries are poisons; you are a murderer. Shall we keep men in a fool's paradise? Shall we lull them into soft slumbers from which they will awake in hell? Are we to become helpers of their damnation by our smooth speeches? In the name of God we will not.[2]

This urgency is why I continue to show people why they need to repent of their sins and turn to Jesus.

RAY [TO BOSS]: Can we just finish up with this?

BOSS: Sure.

RAY: Oh, you're very kind. Thank you for that.

RAY [TO ANISSA]: I couldn't figure why you were laughing because it's the most serious thing in the world I just said to you. So let me say it again.

ANISSA: Okay.

RAY: Sin is so serious to God; he's paying you in death for your sins. The Bible says, "The wages of sin is death" [Romans 6:23]. It's like a judge in a court of law looks at a criminal who's committed multiple crimes. He's murdered young ladies, and the judge says, "I'm going to pay you in the death sentence. This is your wages; this is what's due to you." And sin is so serious to God; he's given us the death sentence. We're on death row, waiting to die because we've violated his law, and if you die in your sins, the Bible warns you'll end up in hell. It says that all liars will have their part in the lake of fire—no thief, no blasphemer, no adulterer will inherit God's kingdom [see Revelation 21:8; 1 Corinthians 6:9–10]. So, can you see that you're in big trouble with God?

ANISSA: Yes.

RAY [TO MAN]: And what about you? Can you see you're in big trouble?

MAN: Yes.

RAY [TO ANISSA]: Now this brings us to "Jesus loves you." I'm going show you *how much*

God loves you. God became a perfect human being two thousand years ago and suffered and died on the cross to take the punishment for the sin of the world. Now you probably know that. Is that right?

ANISSA: Yes.

I am often corrected in the comments section of our YouTube channel when I say that God became a perfect human being in Jesus Christ. They say, "Didn't Jesus call himself the *Son* of God?" While that's true, the Scriptures are very clear that in Christ, the Creator made one special body for himself for the purpose of offering the ultimate sacrifice:

> And without controversy great is the mystery of godliness:
> God was manifested in the flesh,
> Justified in the Spirit,
> Seen by angels,
> Preached among the Gentiles,
> Believed on in the world,
> Received up in glory. (1 Timothy 3:16)

Almighty God, the Creator of the universe, prepared a body for himself and filled that body as a hand fills a glove. Jesus was the express image of the invisible God (see Colossians 1:15; Hebrews 1:3). Look at how all things were made by Jesus: "In the beginning was the Word, and the Word was with God, and the Word was God. He was in the beginning with God. All things were made through Him, and without Him nothing was made that was made…And the Word became flesh and dwelt among us, and we beheld His glory, the glory as of the only begotten of the Father, full of grace and truth" (John 1:1–3, 14).

> RAY: You may not know this: the Ten Commandments are called the moral law. You and I broke the law; Jesus paid the fine. That's what happened on that cross. That's why he said, "It is finished," just before he died [John 19:30]. That means God can *legally* dismiss your case, like a judge can let you go if someone pays your fine. In court, if you've got speeding fines and someone pays them, a judge can say "You're out of here; the fine's been paid by another." God can dismiss your case, forgive your sins, all because Jesus paid the fine in his life's blood. This is what the Bible says: "God proved his love toward us in that while we were yet sinners, Christ died for us" [Romans 5:8, author's paraphrase]. That's *how much* Jesus loves you. He gave up his life so you could live forever.

He was bruised for our iniquities, then he rose from the dead and defeated death, and all you have to do to find everlasting life is repent of your sins and trust in Jesus—like you trust a parachute. If you're going to jump out of a plane, you wouldn't trust your arms to save you. You can flap your arms all you want, but it's not going to work. You trust the parachute. So, simply transfer your trust from yourself to the Savior, and the minute you do that, God will grant you the gift of everlasting life. Now I see you've been smiling a lot. Why is that? Do you believe what I'm saying or just think I'm a bit crazy?

ANISSA: No. I really like this interview actually.

RAY: So, you're going to think about what we talked about?

ANISSA: I...definitely.

RAY [TO MAN]: You're going to think about it too?

MAN: Yes.

RAY [TO ANISSA]: That is so nice to hear. Now do you understand when someone says, "God loves you," that love was expressed in the cross? So I never say to someone "Jesus loves you" because it doesn't make sense. But once you say we were sinners and Christ died on the cross for our sins, that shows how much he loves us.

RAY [TO MAN]: Do you have a Bible at home?

MAN: Yes, I do.

RAY: Okay, can I give you a gift? [Gives them the Gospel of John]

Being a Christian is very frustrating. We say, "We have found eternal life!" In fact, to say that the gospel is good news is the understatement of eternity. And yet most, when told of the unspeakable gift, are ho-hum when they should break down in tears of joy. There seems to be a hint of that same frustration in the opening chapter of Isaiah 53. The famous chapter begins, "Who has believed our report? And to whom has the arm of the LORD been revealed?" (v. 1). Many reject Jesus despite his being "wounded for our transgressions" (v. 5). Still, we are never discouraged in our labor. Just a little frustrated that more don't truly believe.

CHAPTER 3

WITNESSING TO JEWS

The immediate concern when we find out that someone is Jewish is that there will be inevitable offense when we mention Jesus. However, I have found that this concern is almost always groundless if I present the gospel biblically. If you leave out the law, the gospel will be senseless and often offensive to both Jews and non-Jews. But show any human being their sins through the law, leaving him or her hopeless and helpless, and you will more than likely have a listening ear. When I began this conversation with Barry and his friend, I had no idea that he was Jewish or that his friend was a Christian.

> BARRY'S FRIEND: My belief is everybody is going to exist forever. Some people are going to be with God, and some people are going to be without God.

I couldn't help but suspect that this man had a problem with saying the word *hell*. That is understandable in today's climate of so-called tolerance. Many don't want to believe such a place exists. However, Jesus didn't hesitate to say the word, and neither should we: "If your right eye causes you to sin, pluck it out and cast it from you; for it is more profitable for you that one of your members perish, than for your whole body to be cast into hell. And if your right hand causes you to sin, cut it off and cast it from you; for it is more profitable for you that one of your members perish, than for your whole body to be cast into hell" (Matthew 5:29–30).

Besides, why would we avoid using the word if we are trying to awaken sinners to their fearful fate? Would we avoid the word *fire* if someone is asleep while flames were burning their house? That's the very word that will cause them to get up and run. We should, however, always be careful to watch our tone when speaking of the reality of hell. It's been well-said that if they can't see tears in our eyes, they should be able to hear tears in our voice.

RAY: You mean heaven and hell?

BARRY'S FRIEND: Yes.

RAY: Barry, do you agree with that?

BARRY: I agree that there's an afterlife, yes. There's a heaven.

RAY: You're going to heaven?

BARRY: I hope so.

His hope that he would go to heaven gave me hope that he would listen to the gospel. Such talk from him revealed humility. It revealed both a lack of assurance and a longing for salvation. This is why the question "Do you think there is an afterlife?" is so effective. It's inoffensive, and it quickly elicits a valuable response. It's always helpful to have knowledge of the soil in which we are wanting to sow.

RAY: Do you think God is happy with you or angry at you?

This question is effective in quickly revealing the sin of idolatry. When most of us think of idolatry, we think of a graven image to which people bow down. However, idolatry is making up a god in your own image. It may be physical, or it may be in your mind. It is creating a false god that has no sense of justice, righteousness, or truth. It is usually a god that condones sin. In reality, that God doesn't exist. It's a figment of the imagination—the place of imagery.

Rarely will lost people say that God is angry with them. And yet that is the reality of their state. Psalm 7 says, "God is a just judge, and God is angry with the wicked every day" (v. 11).

It is because God is a just judge that he is angry with the wicked. Even in our sinful state, most of us are angered by evil. When I think about what happened to eleven million human beings at the hands of the monster Adolf Hitler, I am infuriated by such wickedness. How much more must a holy God be angered by rape, murder, torture, and all the other evils that are so prevalent in this wicked world!

If we remove his judicial nature, we are left with an unjust Creator, and it would then make sense that he wouldn't be angered by evil. Idolatry is a subtle sin that deceives multitudes. Subtle because it's not an obvious sin but one that leads to others. Note how it is carefully placed in Scripture, right in with sexual sins, just after the warning not to be deceived: "Do you not know that the unrighteous will not inherit the kingdom of God? Do not be deceived. Neither fornicators, nor idolaters, nor adulterers, nor homosexuals, nor sodomites, nor thieves, nor covetous, nor drunkards, nor revilers, nor extortioners will inherit the kingdom of God" (1 Corinthians 6:9–10).

For people to indulge in the pleasures of sexual sin, they have to rid themselves of the restraint of the fear of God. Idolatry will do that.

BARRY: Oh, I have a very loving God.

RAY: You have a very loving God?

BARRY: Yes, I do.

RAY: Is he sweet and cuddly?

BARRY: At some times.

Predictably, Barry revealed that he's guilty of the sin of idolatry. He has his own concept of God. To him, God is *very* loving, inferring that anger isn't part of God's character. He's sometimes sweet and cuddly, like a harmless puppy. Look at how Psalm 7 further describes God's divine wrath: "If [the wicked person] does not turn back, He will sharpen His sword; He bends His bow and makes it ready" (v. 12).

Again, it is because he is just that he's angry. And his anger is pictured as a fearful, sharpened sword and a bent bow ready to thrust an arrow into the heart of the wicked. Wrath "abides" on the sinner. It doesn't go away but rather stores up like a gathering and fearsome storm:

> But because of your callous stubbornness and unrepentant heart you are [deliberately] storing up wrath for yourself on the day of wrath when God's righteous judgment will be revealed. He will pay back to each person according to his deeds [justly, as his deeds deserve]: to those who by persistence in doing good seek [unseen but certain heavenly] glory, honor, and immortality, [He will give the gift of] eternal life. But for those who are selfishly ambitious and self-seeking and

disobedient to the truth but responsive to wickedness, [there will be] wrath and indignation. There will be tribulation and anguish [torturing confinement] for every human soul who does [or permits] evil, to the Jew first and also to the Greek. (Romans 2:5–9 AMP)

But even if Barry was at this point confronted with these verses, he could hold on to his puppy because he wouldn't consider himself to be wicked. There would be no concern. He needed the law of God to show him his sin. That was where I wanted to take the conversation.

RAY: Have you been born again?

BARRY: No, I haven't. I'm Jewish, and I know that most people who are Jewish don't believe in a heaven and a hell, but I do.

RAY: I'm Jewish too.

BARRY: Okay, well, there you go.

My mother was Jewish, which qualifies me to say that I'm Jewish. Some people can't reconcile the fact that someone can be a Christian and a Jew. I'm Christian by religion and Jewish by birth. This often comes in handy when I'm speaking to a Jewish person because it means that they're perhaps going to feel less intimidated. This was perhaps the apostle Paul's attitude:

For though I am free from all men, I have made myself a servant to all, that I might win the more; and to the Jews I became as a Jew, that I might win Jews; to those who are under the law, as under the law, that I might win those who are under the law; to those who are without law, as without law (not being without law toward God, but under law toward Christ), that I might win those who are without law; to the weak I became as weak, that I might win the weak. I have become all things to all men, that I might by all means save some. (1 Corinthians 9:19–22)

Even if you aren't Jewish, don't panic over the thought that when someone says they are Jewish, you are going to have to argue with a person who has the biblical knowledge of Saul of Tarsus. In my experience, many contemporary Jews are not as familiar with the Bible as we may expect. And since a Jewish person might take offense or disregard you when you mention the words of Jesus, start instead with the Ten Commandments. In short, just share the gospel with a Jew as you would with anyone else. This is because it is not our eloquence but rather the gospel that is the power of God unto salvation (see Romans 1:16).

RAY: And the Old Testament says God will turn all nations who forget him into hell [see Psalm

9:17]. So there is a hell according to the Old Testament. When you do something morally wrong, does it anger God?

BARRY: I don't believe any of that. I believe he looks at it and says there are certain lessons that I have to learn in this particular lifetime.

Here was further confirmation of his idolatry. He thought that sin is a lesson. When a man rapes a woman, he is learning lessons. The same applies to thieves, liars, and murderers. Such a philosophy is easily shown to be fallacious—with a little reasoning.

RAY: Is God happy with Hitler?

BARRY: That's unfortunately way above my pay grade. I don't know.

RAY: Yes you do. Hitler was an evil beast that slaughtered eleven million people.

BARRY: He was indeed.

RAY: Do you believe in hell?

BARRY: I think so. I've been in hell.

RAY: No, I don't mean going through a rough time. I mean a literal place of punishment for sin, like, should Hitler go to hell?

BARRY: My own personal opinion? Yes, I believe he should.

RAY: Of course, if God is good, he must punish a mass murderer and a rapist, but the Bible says [God's] so good he's going to judge us by the law of Moses, which we believe in. Thieves and liars and blasphemers. Do you remember the first of the Ten Commandments?

BARRY: Not offhand.

RAY: Don't make up a false god that you can snuggle up to, which we tend to do. It's called idolatry. Because when you make up your own version of God, you can do anything you morally want to. That's what we tend to do. We gravitate to idolatry as a moth does to a flame, and I was an idolater before I was a Christian. Do you think you're a good person morally?

BARRY: Yes.

Both experience and Scripture have shown me that Barry was almost certainly going to tell me that he is a good person: "Most men will proclaim each his own goodness" (Proverbs 20:6).

Plus, I already know that his idolatry had given him a false hope that all is well between him and God. He's good, and God is happy. Once again, he needed the light of the law to show him that his Creator is nothing like what Barry conceived him to be.

RAY: How many lies have you told in your life?

BARRY: I don't know. Probably thousands.

RAY: Ever stolen something?

BARRY: Yes.

RAY: Have you ever used God's name in vain?

BARRY: Of course.

RAY: Would you use your mother's name as a cuss word? You hit your thumb with a hammer, and you want to express disgust. You may use a filth word. Would you use your mother's name in its place? Would you equate the two?

BARRY: I would not want to, no.

RAY: Because you love your mother. You honor her. But you don't love and honor God because you've used his name in place of that filth word.

BARRY: I have in the past.

Sinners predictably try to find comfort in that sin was in the past. The inference is that "anything that I've done that was morally wrong was in the past, but all is now well because I have changed. I'm a better person."

RAY: Well, everything's in the past. [Still, this is] called blasphemy. So serious, in the Old Testament, it's punishable by death. One to go, and I appreciate your patience with me, Barry.

Jesus said that if you look at a woman and lust for her, you commit adultery with her in your heart [see Matthew 5:28]. Have you ever looked at a woman with lust?

I just mentioned Jesus to a Jew. The dentist has just touched a raw nerve. Will the patient be angry, or will he remain in the chair? My concern was that he would brush aside what I've said by saying that he is Jewish and that he doesn't give any credibility to Jesus. But, as I have often found (to my relief and delight), it didn't happen. If he had replied that way, I would have said, "The Old Testament tells us that God requires truth in the inward parts [see Psalm 51:6]. He sees your thought life. Have you ever looked at a woman with lust?" But look at Barry's reply:

BARRY: Of course.

RAY: Have you had sex before marriage?

BARRY: Yes.

RAY: Okay. Here's a summation. I'm not judging you; this is for you to judge yourself. You've told me you're a lying, thieving, blasphemous, fornicating adulterer at heart. If God judges you by the Ten Commandments, which are written on your heart via your conscience, on judgment day, are you going to be innocent or guilty?

BARRY: According to that, guilty.

RAY: Heaven or hell?

BARRY: Probably hell.

I was (once again) relieved and delighted that Barry was being open and honest. The law was doing its wonderful work in bringing the knowledge of sin, and then his conscience could do its duty and accuse him. As Romans 3 explains, "Now we know that whatever the law says, it says to those who are under the law, that every mouth may be stopped, and all the world may become guilty before God. Therefore by the deeds of the law no flesh will be justified in His sight, for by the law is the knowledge of sin" (vv. 19–20).

The knowledge of sin and the accusations of conscience produce a legitimate fear of punishment. Barry was realizing that God is justified in being angry with him. It is like saying (with David after he was exposed to the gravity of his own sin):

> For I acknowledge my transgressions,
> and my sin is always before me.
> Against You, You only, have I sinned,
> and done this evil in Your sight—
> that You may be found just when You speak,
> and blameless when You judge. (Psalm 51:3–4)

This is why it's so important to ask people these difficult questions about their sin and eternal fate. Only by acknowledging that they've sinned against a holy God and deserve hell as eternal punishment will they understand their need for Jesus, the Savior.

RAY: Does that concern you?

This was a pivotal moment. Will he be concerned for his eternal salvation? If he is, that means that he'll more than likely open up to the good news of the gospel. It's like you are a doctor explaining to a patient who is convinced he is healthy that he is in reality dying of a terrible disease for which you have a cure. If he becomes convinced and is seriously concerned about his condition, he is going to, more than likely, be very interested in the cure. If Barry is concerned, he will see the gospel as his only hope of salvation and, more than likely, will embrace it.

BARRY: Yes.

RAY: It horrifies me. I've just met you, Barry, but I love you, and the thought of you ending up in hell terrifies me. Do you remember how the children of Israel were delivered from the power of death? The plagues? Remember when death came over? What were they told to do to be safe, do you remember?

Here was where I took a different path than I would with a non-Jew. I was hoping that he was educated in the meaning of the Passover. If he was, that would help the sacrifice of the Lamb of God make sense to him—although he ultimately needs to see Jesus as the Passover lamb. By starting with this lamb, I hoped to avoid offense that could keep him from hearing what I had to say.

BARRY: Put blood on their doors.

RAY: The blood of the lamb. Do you know what John the Baptist said the first time he saw Jesus? Do you remember what he said?

BARRY: I don't know.

RAY: He said, "Behold! The Lamb of God who takes away the sin of the world" [John 1:29]. The way to escape death is to apply the blood of the Lamb that God supplied, and the reason God supplied a sacrificial Lamb was to take the punishment for the sin of the world. Jesus suffered and died on the cross, and the last words he spoke just before he dismissed his spirit were "It is finished" [John 19:30]. We broke God's law, the Ten Commandments. Jesus paid the fine. That's what happened on that cross. It was God's sacrifice so that you and I could have our case dismissed.

If you're in court and someone pays your fine, a judge can actually let you go and say, "This fine's been paid by someone else. It was a stack of speeding fines, but they're paid; you're out of here." He can do that which is legal and right and just. Barry, God can forgive your sins. He can let you live forever, legally, all because Jesus paid the fine in his life's blood. He was the Messiah, the Lamb of God who suffered for the sin of the world, rose again on the third day, and defeated death. And if you'll simply repent of your sins, turn from them and trust in Jesus (don't trust your goodness—it's not going to work on the day of judgment—just trust in the Savior), you've got a promise from the God who cannot lie that he'll grant you everlasting life as a free gift. Are you going to think about what we talked about?

BARRY: Absolutely.

What a joy and relief it was for me to hear that word. There was no offense when I mentioned Jesus.

RAY: "Absolutely"? You're going to think about it with a sense of seriousness, as if you could die tonight at midnight? How old are you?

BARRY: Seventy-six.

RAY: You don't know when you're going to die. I'm in my seventies, and every night I go to sleep, and I wake up in the morning and say, "Thank you, Lord, I've got another day." You want to have assurance you've got everlasting life, that your sins are forgiven. So please, when you leave here, give this some serious thought. Get before the God who gave you life and say, "I've used your name as a cuss word. I've fornicated. I've lied and stolen. I've sinned against you. Please wash me clean and create a clean heart in me." And God cannot lie. He will grant you that request if you come to him with a contrite heart and are genuinely sorrowful for your sins. Do you have a Bible at home?

BARRY: No.

RAY [TO BARRY'S FRIEND]: Could you give him a Bible?

BARRY'S FRIEND: Sure.

I then asked Barry's friend if he would talk further with Barry about his salvation, which he said he would do if that was Barry's desire.

I'm always honored to speak to Jewish people. I so want them to understand why Jesus is so important. The gospel went to the Jew first because they had the law to help it make sense. The problem is that most

Jewish people nowadays are commonly considered secular Jews. They are merely culturally Jewish. They may not know or believe the Scriptures. Yet the knowledge that someone is Jewish should not stop us from explaining to them the saving works of Jesus.

CHAPTER 4

DEATH AND THE AFTERLIFE

The greatest benefit for the Christian is the fact that death has lost its sting. In Christ, we are legally saved from death's power because he paid our fine on the cross. We're not only saved from the power of death, but we are also saved from the *fear* of death. God has given us something to help us conquer that haunting terror that grips every human being before they come to Christ. Our faith in Jesus, like having faith in a parachute, lifts us above our fears. So our fear will be in direct proportion to how much faith we have. If we have great faith in a parachute, we'll have little fear when we jump.

This chapter contains two encounters. One is with a woman in her late fifties named Lisa, who had recently lost her husband, and the other is with Nancy, who was in her early twenties.

I knew about Lisa losing her husband before we turned the cameras on and, therefore, took her tragic situation into account. Sharing the gospel with someone who has just lost a loved one is a little unnerving. This is because I don't want to insinuate that the person she just lost will end up in hell. Going to hell, whether ourselves or our loved ones, is a very real concern for most of us. However, I have found that when an unsaved person has a death in the family, it not only grieves them. It also scares them and makes them wonder what will happen to them when they pass on. I, therefore, have to discipline myself to be sensitive to the loss but, at the same time, direct my attention and my concern to the living.

RAY: Are you afraid of dying?

LISA: Not anymore.

RAY: Why aren't you afraid?

LISA: Because that's the next stage, and my husband just died. I've been getting signs from him, so I feel it's not as bad as we think it is.

This dear lady had lost her precious husband and had found comfort in either imaginary signs or in coincidences or perhaps in familiar spirits. I could have asked what these signs were but didn't so Lisa would stay open to our conversation. At the time, I was producing a video on George Harrison, a member of the Beatles who may have come to faith in Jesus on his deathbed. George Harrison once said, "Everything else can wait, but the search for God cannot wait."[3] In "My Sweet Lord," one of his famous songs, he said how much he wanted to be in the presence of the Lord. As a Hare Krishna, he was clearly unsatisfied and still desperately searching for God.

I remembered the promise of God in Jeremiah 29:13: "And you will seek Me and find Me, when you search for Me with all your heart." In my research for a book I wrote called *The Beatles, God and the Bible*, I sadly concluded that George didn't come to Christ, that he died in his sins. But I may have gotten it wrong because of what I have uncovered since then. A comment on our YouTube channel spoke of his conversion to Christ, which I then investigated.

As it turns out, while Emerson Fittipaldi, a retired racing driver and born-again Christian, was speaking to a church, he mentioned his long-time friendship with George Harrison and said, "When he was very sick, I ask[ed] for a pastor in Brazil to fly to Switzerland. [George] was [in a] hospital in Switzerland. And I went to see him for two days...and we prayed, and [George] accept[ed] Christ."[4]

And I couldn't be more delighted if I was wrong about George's salvation. I asked Lisa's opinion on the band to introduce the idea of God's importance.

RAY: Do you like the Beatles?

LISA: I *love* the Beatles.

RAY: George Harrison said, "The most important thing in life is to seek God" [author's paraphrase]. Do you agree with him?

LISA: I don't know if it's the most important, but it's *very* important.

RAY: Do you know what made me seek after God? One thing.

LISA: What?

RAY: Death.

LISA: That's true.

Her reaction was very encouraging. I was hoping that she had been thinking about God and the issues of life and death. Another concern I have is that someone who has lost a loved one could be bitter at God for the loss, and the bitterness would be a barrier. But not so with Lisa.

While some might find a sense of comfort in bitterness, it is futile to be bitter at God—for at least two reasons: God is *always* right, and he is without sin. Even if we cannot understand why his judgment is right, he never makes a wrong judgment. So any bitterness against him would be misdirected. However, those who are grieving may not be ready to hear this yet, and we want to extend a compassionate heart to those experiencing loss.

RAY: It's a good reason to seek God because he's eternal. He has no beginning, no end. He's the author and source of life itself, and if we want to find everlasting life, we've somehow got to find God. Do you ever read the Bible?

LISA: A while ago. It's been a while.

RAY: Do you know what the Bible says death actually is?

LISA: No.

RAY: It's wages.

LISA: Really?

RAY: Yes. Romans 6:23 says, "The wages of sin is death." That means God is paying you in death for your sins. It's like a judge in a court of law looks at a heinous criminal who's murdered three girls after he raped them and says, "You've earned the death sentence. This is your wages. This is what's due to you. This is what we're going to pay you." Sin is so serious to a holy God that he's given us the death sentence—capital punishment. Do you think you are evil enough, sinful enough, for God to put you to death for your sins?

LISA: That is a good question. I would have to think about that one, but I don't think I've done anything *that* bad.

RAY: You know how to tell if you have?

LISA: How?

RAY: Just look at the Ten Commandments.

LISA: Oh yes, I'm good.

RAY: You think you're a good person?

LISA: Yes.

Here was my signpost. Her answer gave me clear directions. She has no knowledge of sin, indicated by her thinking that she's a good person. Here is a dying patient who is convinced that she is perfectly healthy, so I must show her the disease that is going to kill her if she doesn't find the cure. Inwardly, I was praying that Lisa had a good and honest heart, that she would listen to the voice of her conscience as it bore witness with God's law: "When Gentiles, who do not have the law, by nature do the things in the law,…[they] show the work of the law written in their hearts, their conscience also bearing witness, and between themselves their thoughts accusing or else excusing them" (Romans 2:14–15).

RAY: Okay, here's a test. Can you be honest with me?

LISA: I'll try. Yes, I can.

RAY: Ever stolen something?

LISA: Yes, when I was a kid.

RAY: What do you call someone who steals?

LISA: A thief, right?

RAY: So, what are you?

LISA: Well, I *was* a thief.

RAY: A lying thief.

LISA: There you go. Ah.

RAY: Actually, we tend to put our crimes in the past, our sins in the past, but *everything* we do is in the past.

There is something sad and even pathetic to hear grown human beings try to cover their sins. The Bible warns that "he who covers his sins will not prosper, but whoever confesses and forsakes them will have mercy" (Proverbs 28:13). It is so refreshing to hear a sinner come clean before the Lord and acknowledge his or her guilt.

Lisa's "I *was* a thief" showed me that she thought time forgives sin with God. But it doesn't. Peter said, "But, beloved, do not forget this one thing, that with the Lord one day is as a thousand years, and a thousand years as one day" (2 Peter 3:8). Lisa's comment also showed me that she may have been thinking that reformation is equal to washing away sin. The criminal thinks the judge won't prosecute his crime because he's become upright since the bank robbery. Sometimes that works in humanity's court, but God dwells outside of the dimension of time and remembers sin. He sees the sins of our youth as if they were committed yesterday. David cried, "Do not remember the sins of my youth, nor my transgressions; according to Your mercy remember me, for Your goodness' sake, O LORD" (Psalm 25:7).

My goal then was to keep revealing Lisa's sin nature so she could understand the importance of Jesus' sacrifice on the cross. Only because of Jesus' blood does God forgive and forget the repentant person's sins (see 1 John 1:7–9; Isaiah 43:25–26).

RAY: Have you ever used God's name in vain?

LISA: Yes, and I ask for forgiveness every night.

RAY: Love your mother?

LISA: Yes.

RAY: Would you ever use your *mother's* name as a cuss word?

LISA: No.

RAY: Why not?

LISA: Because it's my mom.

RAY: You'd never insult her by doing that, would you?

LISA: No.

RAY: But you have done it with God's name, and he gave you your mother. He gave you your life and every blessing you've ever had, and his name is holy. You've actually substituted it for a filth word…to express disgust. Lisa, that's called blasphemy; it's very serious in his eyes, and you already know that. Now Jesus said that if you look with lust, you commit adultery in your heart [see Matthew 5:28]. Have you ever looked with lust?

Lisa was really sweet, and inside I was dying. I wanted to get beyond her sin and talk about the love of God, but I dared not do so. Not yet. She must see her disease, or she would never appreciate or appropriate the cure. I wanted her to thirst after righteousness, and she wouldn't do that unless she saw that she desperately needed God's mercy. So I ignored my selfish fears.

RAY: Lisa, I'm not judging you. This is for you to judge yourself. This is for you to make the call. You've told me you're a lying thief, a blasphemer, and an adulterer at heart. If God judges you by those Ten Commandments on judgment day, are you going to be innocent or guilty?

LISA: I'm going to be guilty.

RAY: So, you've *earned* your wages.

LISA: I have.

Oh, the wonderful sound of an honest heart! This is King David coming clean. David had committed adultery and murder, and God sent Nathan the prophet to reprove him for his sin. Notice (in the following verses) that Nathan didn't generalize David's sin. He was specific. This is because David needed to see his sin as being a crime against God. Only knowing that would cause him to tremble. So Nathan directed the king's gaze toward heaven:

> "Why have you despised the commandment of the LORD, to do evil in His sight? You have killed Uriah the Hittite with the sword; you have taken his wife to be your wife, and have killed him with the sword of the people of Ammon. Now therefore, the sword shall never depart from your house, because you have despised Me, and have taken the wife of Uriah the Hittite to be your wife." Thus says the LORD: "Behold, I will raise up adversity against you from your own house; and I will take your wives before

your eyes and give them to your neighbor, and he shall lie with your wives in the sight of this sun. For you did it secretly, but I will do this thing before all Israel, before the sun."

So David said to Nathan, "I have sinned against the LORD."

And Nathan said to David, "The LORD also has put away your sin; you shall not die." (2 Samuel 12:9–13)

It was only when David admitted that he had sinned against God that Nathan gave him the good news of mercy. And Lisa's "I have [earned my wages]" showed me that she was ready for the good news of the gospel. She was ready to hear about Jesus.

RAY: So, what can you do to avoid the damnation of hell? How can you be made right with God?

LISA: That's a good question as well.

RAY: It's the big question. It's what George Harrison sought after. He devoted himself to trying to find the answer to that. It was actually right under his nose. It's under yours too. Jesus died on the cross for the sin of the world. You've heard that?

LISA: Yes.

RAY: Most people have, but they don't understand it—and it can change everything. If you
can get a grip of this, it'll change everything for
you. The Ten Commandments, that which we've
just looked at, are called the moral law. You
and I broke the law. Jesus paid the fine. Do you
remember his last words on the cross? He said
three very profound words.

LISA: No.

RAY: He said, "It is finished" [John 19:30].
That's a weird thing to say as you're dying. But
he was saying that the debt has been paid. We
broke God's law; Jesus paid the fine. It's like if
you're in a court of law and you've gotten a lot
of speeding fines, the judge could say, "This is
very serious, but someone's paid these fines.
You're out of here." He can let you go if someone
pays your fine. And he can still do that which is
legal and right and just. And God can take the
death sentence off you. He can *legally* dismiss
your case, all because Jesus paid the fine in his
life's blood. He can grant you everlasting life as
a free gift—not because you're good but because
he's good, and he's rich in mercy.

After Jesus suffered for our sins, he
rose from the dead and defeated your greatest

enemy, death itself. The Bible says it was not possible that death could hold him [see Acts 2:24], and all you have to do to find everlasting life is repent of your sins. It's more than just confessing them; it's turning from sin. You can't say, "I'm a Christian," but you fornicate and lie and steal and blaspheme. You've got to be genuine in your repentance, and then you trust in Jesus. Now, let me ask you a question. Lisa, if you're on the edge of a plane ten thousand feet up, why would you put on a parachute?

LISA: To live.

RAY: You don't want to die. You don't want to hit the ground at 120 miles an hour. Your motivation is fear, and in that case, fear is your friend. It's not your enemy. It's causing you to put on a parachute, and what I've tried to do with you—and thank you for your patience—is I've tried to put the fear of God on you because "the fear of God is the beginning of wisdom," according to the Bible [Proverbs 9:10, author's paraphrase]. And, in that case, fear is your friend, not your enemy, because it'll drive you the mercy of God in Christ—where you'll find everlasting life.

You're like someone on the edge of plane ten thousand feet up, and this is your plan: you're going to flap your arms and try to save yourself when you jump. I'd say, "Don't do that, Lisa. Trust the parachute!" It's as simple as that. Don't trust yourself; trust the parachute. So, don't trust your goodness to save you on judgment day. Trust the Savior; transfer your faith from yourself to the Savior. Is this making sense?

LISA: Yes, it is.

RAY: You're going to think about what we talked about?

LISA: I am.

RAY: You're going to repent and trust Christ?

LISA: I'm going to.

RAY: Can I pray with you?

LISA: Sure.

RAY: Father, I thank you for Lisa. I thank you for her open heart and her honesty in admitting her sins. I pray today she'll understand your love expressed in the cross and find a place of genuine repentance and faith in Jesus and pass from death to life because of your mercy. In Jesus' name we pray, amen.

LISA: Amen.

RAY: I've got a gift for you.

LISA: Okay.

RAY: A couple of gifts.

LISA: Okay.

RAY: This is a book I wrote called *The Beatles, God and the Bible*, and you're a Beatles fan.

LISA: I am.

RAY: This is *How to Be Free from the Fear of Death*, and it'll really help you grow in your faith.

LISA: Thank you.

Because of her questions about death, Lisa was more willing to hear how Jesus' sacrifice defeated death and made a way for our salvation.

In a conversation with a young woman I encountered, I began with a similar question about death and the afterlife that I had asked Lisa. Even though, to my knowledge, Nancy hadn't lost someone close to her recently, she was humble and wide-eyed right from the beginning of the conversation. I couldn't help but feel that God had led me to speak with her.

RAY: So where do people go when they die?

NANCY: Some people go to heaven, and some people go with the, um…

RAY: Are you scared to say the word *hell*?

NANCY: Hell. Yes.

RAY: Where are *you* going?

NANCY: Well, I think I'm not going to heaven because I'm not doing the correct things that we're supposed to be doing.

RAY: What do you have to do to go to heaven?

NANCY: Help people; be a good person.

RAY: How many people do you have to help to get to heaven? Ten? One hundred? Five hundred?

NANCY: Ten people will be good.

RAY: You know, the Bible says something different.

NANCY: I don't read the Bible, like, that often.

RAY: You should, because do you know what it says? It says you don't get to heaven by being good. How many lies have you told in your life?

NANCY: Oh. [Laughs] A lot.

RAY: Have you ever used God's name in vain?

NANCY: Yes, sometimes.

RAY: His name is holy, and you've used as a cuss word. Have you ever looked at someone with lust?

NANCY: Yes.

RAY: Have you had sex before marriage?

NANCY: Oh yes.

RAY: If God judges you by those Ten Commandments on judgment day, are you going to be innocent or guilty?

NANCY: Guilty.

RAY: Heaven or hell?

NANCY: I say hell.

RAY: Now, does that concern you?

NANCY: Yes, in some way.

RAY: Man, it concerns me big-time. I've just met you, but I care about you. I don't want you to go to hell.

NANCY: I'm always, you know, talking with God when I'm alone and telling him I'm sorry for doing this during the day, during the night.

RAY: Well, maybe today God's answered your prayers by me sharing the gospel with you on how to be saved. You repent and trust alone in Jesus. The minute you do that you've got God's promise he'll grant you everlasting life as a free gift, and the Bible says God cannot lie. He's without sin, so you can trust him with all your heart. When he says it, he means it. He'll keep his promise. He'll grant you everlasting life as a free gift. Do you believe what I'm saying?

NANCY: Yes.

RAY: You're going to think about what we talked about?

NANCY: Yes.

RAY: You're going to repent and trust in Jesus?

NANCY: Yes.

RAY: Can I pray for you?

NANCY: Yes, it's fine.

RAY: Father, I pray for Nancy. Thank you for her open heart. I pray she'll think about her secret sins and how serious sin is in your eyes and today repent and trust alone in Jesus and be born again with a new heart and new desires all because of your mercy. In Jesus' name we pray, amen.

NANCY: Amen.

My heart sure went out to Nancy. And I was so thankful that she was open to the gospel. I couldn't help but think that it was her fear of death that opened her heart to what I had to say.

If you are aware of the traditions of modern Christianity, you may be asking why it is that I don't lead penitent sinners in what is commonly called the sinner's prayer. Why don't I close the deal? Here's why. When I became a Christian way back in 1972, I did great damage to the cause of the kingdom by leading prospective converts in the sinner's prayer. Because they didn't really understand what they were doing, they didn't seek the Lord with their own hearts or recognize their need to turn from their sin.

The sinner's prayer isn't biblical. It's not found in Scripture. This modern method is perhaps the number one reason why the contemporary church is filled with false converts (tares among the wheat and goats among the sheep) and why 80–90 percent of those who come to Christianity through this doorway fall away from the faith.

Here is an email from someone who thought he was saved after praying the sinner's prayer:

> Thank you so much, Ray, for your faithfulness in presenting the gospel along with the law! I always assumed I was saved simply because I prayed the sinner's prayer, but I never thought of myself as a sinner. I could not see my own sin. I was so blinded by pride, ego, selfishness, and self-centeredness that I was deceived and didn't even realize it. If you would have asked me six years ago, I would have said yes, I was a Christian, but

everything I did was for my glory and not the Lord. I was so lost and didn't even know it.

I was led by God's Holy Spirit (I believe) to your YouTube channel. It was then and only then that I came to realize the terminal condition of my soul. I saw myself for the very first time as the lost wretch that I was. I saw the need for repentance. I saw my sin for what it was—a death sentence if left unchecked. It was because of the moral law that was presented to me in such a unique and powerful way that I truly understood my spiritual condition and the need to put on the Lord Jesus as I would put on a parachute.

It's not about what I've done. But it's all about what Jesus did for me on that cross two thousand years ago. I was bought and paid for with the price of Christ's precious blood. My life is no longer my own. And I never want to shame the name of my Lord and Savior Jesus Christ ever again. He has changed me so much that I hardly recognize myself any longer. He has given me a new heart and a new mind, and daily he is conforming me into his likeness. I'm so incredibly grateful to him for saving a wretch like me. He accepted me just as I was; I didn't need to clean up my act. Praise the Lord. He has made me a brand-new creation (2 Corinthians 5:17).

What a magnificent testimony of the power of Jesus' blood on the cross! Yet this person didn't realize his sin nature—and the life-changing reality of Jesus' death and resurrection—by simply praying a prayer. He needed to see his sin revealed by the law.

Perhaps you're thinking, *But what about all those who were genuinely saved who prayed the sinner's prayer?* I address that issue in a book called *God Has a Wonderful Plan for Your Life: The Myth of the Modern Message:*[5]

> Imagine that someone invented a parachute that was 100 percent trustworthy; the chute opened every time, without exception, and got the wearer safely to the ground. The key was to diligently follow the manufacturer's instructions. Now imagine that the packers began to ignore the instructions and use a new "fast-and-easy" method of folding that greatly increased production. Everyone rejoiced that so much time and effort could now be saved.
>
> As time passed, however, it became evident that something was radically wrong. They discovered that nine out of every ten people who jumped with the "fast-folded" parachutes fell to their deaths!

What would you say to someone who ignored the 90 percent of dead, mangled bodies on the ground, and pointed to the 10 percent "success" rate for justification of their methods? The "God has a wonderful plan" method is easy—but it is also devastating. As we will see, we have tampered with the instructions on how to reach the lost, with dire eternal consequences.[6]

This is a matter of death or life. When dealing with someone's eternal fate, we shouldn't be aiming for fast and easy, telling them that God has a wonderful plan for them as long as they repeat a specific prayer, but rather, we should commend people to God. True repentance flows from the hearts of people who have truly recognized their sin; they don't need you to tell them what to say. Always remember that it's God who saves, not us.

CHAPTER 5

THE NECESSITY OF NEW BIRTH

I have been told by a number of Roman Catholics not to witness to Catholics who say they haven't been born again. This is because they believe that they were born again when they were christened (baptized) as a baby and that their position in the church was further strengthened through confirmation as an older child or teenager. However, if christening itself does not "produce fruit that is consistent with repentance [demonstrating new behavior that proves a change of heart, and a conscious decision to turn away from sin]" (Matthew 3:8 AMP), then they are unsaved, and if they die in their sins, they will end up in hell. So this is no small issue.

In a similar way, many Protestants believe they don't need to be witnessed to because they grew up in church. Maybe their parents brought them to church every Sunday, and today they believe God exists and, therefore, call themselves Christians. But is that what it means to be born again? Not according to Matthew 3:8. Protestants are more familiar with the term "born again," and so these people might even say yes if I ask them whether they are born again. But it only takes me a few questions to realize they're not living in faith. They don't have a relationship with God. They're not trusting in what Jesus did on the cross for them.

Whether people call themselves Catholic or Protestant or atheistic, it breaks my heart that they haven't been born again. So the question arises, does being "born again" mean to be baptized in water? Many believe that it does, and they base that conviction on the words of Jesus: "Most assuredly, I say to you, unless one is born of water and the Spirit, he cannot enter the kingdom of God. That which is born of the flesh is flesh, and that which is born of the Spirit is spirit. Do not marvel that I said to you, 'You must be born again'" (John 3:5–7).

It's always wise to interpret Scripture with Scripture. Listen to what Peter said about baptism: "Then Peter said unto them, Repent, and be baptized every one of you in the name of Jesus Christ for the remission of sins, and ye shall receive the gift of the Holy Ghost" (Acts 2:38 KJV). He said to *repent* and be baptized. An infant can't repent because he or she has no knowledge of sin. So John 3 isn't speaking of infant baptism.

In this passage of John, Jesus says that we must be "born of water and the Spirit" (v. 5). Notice that he spoke of being born of water first, which refers to the fact that we are all born into this world surrounded by water—a liquid called amniotic fluid. Then he further confirms that the reference to water is natural to human birth by saying, "That which is born of the flesh is flesh [natural birth], and that which is born of the Spirit is spirit [spiritual birth]" (v. 6).

Again, these two are differentiated. We are all born of the flesh, surrounded by water. That's our first birth that ushers us into this world. But Jesus said that each of us *must* be born again. We must be born of the Spirit to enter the kingdom of heaven. This comes through repentance and faith alone in Jesus for our eternal salvation.

Why would we deny *anyone* who hasn't been born again the chance to hear the gospel? Just because people tell me that they are Catholic or that they are already a Christian, I'm not going to say, "Okay. I'll not tell you how to find everlasting life. That disqualifies you." I won't give up until I've spoken with them long enough to see whether they have a real relationship with God or whether they're just claiming the label "Christian" and trusting in a few traditions from childhood.

Isabella was a young woman I spoke to who told me she was raised in the Catholic Church. Because she didn't say she was born again, I prepared to take her through the Ten Commandments, just like I would with anyone else who did not trust in Christ alone for salvation.

> RAY: Now, let's go back to the commandments and see how you're going to do on judgment day. Can you handle that?
>
> ISABELLA: Let's do it.
>
> RAY: Can you be honest with me?
>
> ISABELLA: I will.
>
> RAY: Is God first in your life?
>
> ISABELLA: He is.
>
> RAY: You love him with heart, mind, soul, and strength and love your neighbor as much as you love yourself?
>
> ISABELLA: I do.
>
> RAY: Have you ever used God's name in vain?
>
> ISABELLA: I have.
>
> RAY: Would you use your mother's name as a cuss word?

ISABELLA: No, I would not.

RAY: Why not?

ISABELLA: Because I respect that woman, you know. She birthed me. She raised me to who I am today, and I would never do that.

RAY: But you don't respect God because you've taken this holy name that godly Jews won't even speak because it's so holy and substitute it for [a cuss] word. That's what it means to take it in vain, to give it no honor. So, you don't love God with heart, mind, soul, and strength. So you've broken the first and the third.

ISABELLA: I know.

RAY: How many lies have you told in your life?

ISABELLA: [Laughs] Oh, I couldn't tell you that.

RAY: Quite a few?

ISABELLA: Quite a few.

RAY: So, what do you call someone who tells lies.

ISABELLA: A liar.

RAY: Have you ever stolen something in your whole life, even if it's small?

ISABELLA: I have.

RAY: What do you call someone who steals?

ISABELLA: A thief.

RAY: So, what are you?

ISABELLA: A thief.

RAY: No, you're not. You're a lying thief.

ISABELLA: [Laughs] Yes.

RAY: I'm going to go a little personal here. I hope you can handle it. Jesus said that if you look was lust, you commit adultery in the heart [see Matthew 5:28]. Have you ever looked with lust?

ISABELLA: I have, yes.

RAY: Have you had sex before marriage?

ISABELLA: I have.

RAY: So, Isabella, here's the summation. This is for you; it's not for me. I wouldn't judge you. I don't have that right. But you've told me you're a lying, thieving, blasphemous, fornicating adulterer at heart. So, if you face God on judgment day and he judges you by those commandments, which the Bible says he will, will you be innocent or guilty?

ISABELLA: I would be guilty.

RAY: Heaven or hell?

ISABELLA: It would be hell.

RAY: Now, does that concern you?

ISABELLA: It does, yes.

RAY: It concerns me; it breaks my heart, the thought of you ending up in hell. You know what the Bible says death actually is?

ISABELLA: What is it?

RAY: Wages.

ISABELLA: Wages?

RAY: Ever heard of the Bible verse, "The wages of sin is death" [Romans 6:23]?

ISABELLA: I have.

RAY: Death is wages. It's like a judge in a court of law looks at a heinous criminal who has raped three girls and murdered them, and he says, "You've earned the death sentence. This is your wages. This is what is due to you. This is what we're paying you." And sin is so serious in the eyes of a holy God that he's given us the death sentence. "The soul [who] sins shall die" [Ezekiel 18:20]. He's given us capital punishment.

We think lightly of sin. A little blasphemy, we can't help it, taking God's name in vain, a few lies here and there, stealing. The second part of that verse is "*But* the gift of God is eternal life through Jesus Christ our Lord" [Romans

6:23, author's paraphrase and emphasis]. What did God do for guilty sinners so we wouldn't have to go to hell, do you know?

ISABELLA: I don't.

RAY: God did something wonderful, but you don't really understand it. You don't know what it is?

ISABELLA: He sacrificed his…you're talking about God, right? He sacrificed his Son.

Most nominal Christians—people who would call themselves Christians but otherwise live no differently from those who are not religious—have a measure of understanding about the cross if they grew up attending church. This knowledge of Jesus' life is a positive because what I'm telling them builds on that which is in their Bible and part of their beliefs. So they shouldn't feel threatened that I'm trying to take them away from their religion.

RAY: Do you understand the legal implications of that?

ISABELLA: Yes.

RAY: Tell me: What are they?

ISABELLA: He loves us.

RAY: Yes, but there's a reason that happened.

ISABELLA: To have life on earth.

RAY: Well, let me put it this way and get your thoughts. The Ten Commandments, that's what we've looked at, are called the moral law. You and I broke the law; Jesus paid the fine. That's what happened on the cross—that's why he said, "It is finished" [John 19:30].

Isabella, if you're in court and someone pays your fine, like your speeding fines, the judge can *legally* let you go. He can say, "These are serious fines, but you're out of here because someone paid them." And God can legally let us live. He can take the death sentence off us because Jesus paid the fine in his life's blood. And then he rose from the dead and defeated death, and all you have to do to find everlasting life is to turn from sin perpetually. Don't play the hypocrite and say, "I'm a Christian," but you lie, steal, fornicate, and blaspheme. That's just deceiving yourself. You've got to be genuine and then trust in Jesus like you'd trust a parachute. Do you know what the fear of God is?

ISABELLA: What is it?

RAY: Well, the Bible says Jesus was heard by God "in that he feared" [Hebrews 5:7 KJV]. The Bible says that the fear of God is the beginning of wisdom [see Proverbs 9:10]; through the fear of the Lord, men depart from sin [see Proverbs 16:6]. What I've tried to do (and I'll qualify this) is put the fear of God in you. If you're going to jump out of a plane and you're going to jump without a parachute because you thought it'd be all right, I'd hang you out of the plane for two minutes by your ankles so you come back in and say, "This is scary! I've *got* to put on a parachute." Fear is your friend if that happens; it's not your enemy. And the fear of God is the beginning of wisdom.

I trust today that you'll see the fear of God—that which I've tried to put in you—as your friend, not your enemy, because it's going to drive you to the cross where you say, "God, I've been lying and blaspheming and fornicating and doing things I know are wrong. Please forgive me, and today I put my trust in Jesus, once and for all, to have my sins forgiven." And the minute you do that, you've got a promise from the God who cannot lie that he will grant you everlasting life instantly as a free gift. You don't have to earn it. You don't deserve it. It comes because he's good, not because we're good— that's called amazing grace, God's unmerited favor toward us because he loves us. He's the lover of our soul. Are you going to think about what we talked about today?

ISABELLA: I am. I will.

RAY: You have a Bible?

ISABELLA: I do.

RAY: When did you last read it?

ISABELLA: When did I last read it? I couldn't give you a time.

RAY: It's God's love letter to you, so when you leave here, in the quietness of your heart, just confess your sins to God and say, "God forgive me; create a clean heart in me," and then trust in Jesus, not your goodness. Trust in Jesus because you don't have goodness. You are like the rest of us. So, make sure your faith is in Jesus and not in yourself. Making sense?

ISABELLA: Making sense.

RAY: You're going to think about this?

ISABELLA: I will.

RAY: Can I give you a book I've written?

ISABELLA: Yes, let's do it.

I share the same message with people of all beliefs and backgrounds: God will grant you his gift of grace and eternal life when you put your faith in Jesus, not yourself. And it is only through Jesus' resurrection that you can be born again: "Blessed be the God and Father of our Lord Jesus Christ, who according to His abundant mercy has begotten us again to a living hope through the resurrection of Jesus Christ from the dead" (1 Peter 1:3). If they have already trusted in Jesus, then I've met a brother or sister in Christ. But if they haven't, I pray God will continue to work in their lives.

CHAPTER 6

THE HUMAN ASSUMPTION

Deroda was a self-confident woman (perhaps in her early thirties) who wasn't hesitant to say that illegal drug usage was a great way to explore our spirituality. It is true that drugs like LSD do open the mind. Back in the late 1950s, the drug was even viewed in a positive light because of this. However, it was soon outlawed because it also proved to be dangerous.

I had a friend who had such a bad trip that she tragically threw herself off a thousand-foot cliff. It seemed that Deroda hadn't read the memo about how dangerous LSD can be. Besides her interest in hallucinogens, Deroda believed that she could determine her own standard of goodness. In other words, she assumed she could make her own ideas about God.

RAY: What are your thoughts on the afterlife?

DERODA: I think that our souls really do go somewhere else into this dimension that we possibly may have explored, I think, through psychedelics and other forms of that type of activity.

RAY: Are you talking about taking LSD to find out what's on the other side?

DERODA: Yes, I'm not sure before I go, but I know it's going to be somewhere incredible and amazing because our souls are too complex to only be stuck in this dimension. I know that I have faith in where I want to go, and being a good person here and the way I fulfill my life and my soul on this earth is going to really transcend where I go afterward.

Some people assume that pleasure after death is our right. It's based on the presumption that God isn't holy; that he is just like us. We all make mistakes, but that's human nature. God is love, they say, and therefore, he will obviously overlook these minor mistakes...which everyone makes. So there's no concern that he would or could send them to hell. The criminal thinks the judge will understand his rape and murder and, therefore, let him go. Such an analogy may seem extreme, but it's not. Sin is so serious to a holy God that he's given the best of us the death sentence and warns that even our good deeds are horribly tainted by sin:

For we all have become like one who is [cere-
monially] unclean [like a leper],
and all our deeds of righteousness are like filthy
rags;
we all wither and decay like a leaf,
and our wickedness [our sin, our injustice,
our wrongdoing], like the wind, takes us away
[carrying us far from God's favor, toward
destruction]. (Isaiah 64:6 AMP)

This presumption that God is just like us and
that all is well comes from not believing the Scriptures.

RAY: So, you are a good person?

DERODA: I like to think so. Absolutely.

RAY: Are you an educated person?

DERODA: Yes.

RAY: Well-read?

DERODA: Well-read.

RAY: What's the biggest-selling book of all
time?

DERODA: I don't know.

RAY: It's the Bible.

DERODA: Oh, that would make sense, yes.

RAY: Do you believe the Bible?

DERODA: I believe the Bible has been rewritten so many times that, at this point, I'm not sure if we even know it was written to begin with.

RAY: Now you're sure of that?

DERODA: Um, yes. It's a game of telephone. We're constantly rewriting it and trying to translate it. And I grew up very religious.

RAY: As a Christian?

DERODA: Yes, in a very Catholic home. My dad is a deacon actually.

RAY: Were you born again?

DERODA: Was I born again?

RAY: Do you know what that is? Jesus said in John chapter 3, unless you're born again, you're not going to enter heaven. It's very, very clear. So, it's important to be born again. When you become born again, you become a Christian. Whether you're Catholic or Protestant, by being born again, you become a Christian. Are you going to make it to heaven? You're a good person? Have you kept the Ten Commandments?

DERODA: I don't think I need to keep the Ten Commandments in order to get into heaven, honestly.

RAY: Really?

DERODA: I've gotten way past that with my religion and my faith in God, where I truly believe that I can't live with my boyfriend before I marry him. I'm not going to get into heaven if I do that. So truthfully, I believe in the Ten Commandments, but I think it takes a lot more for you to get into heaven. All right, test me.

RAY: Okay.

DERODA: I'm ready.

RAY: Are you ready? How many lies have you told in your life?

DERODA: Many.

RAY: What do you call someone who's told many lies?

DERODA: A liar.

RAY: So, what are you?

DERODA: A liar.

RAY: You still think you're a good person?

DERODA: I am.

RAY: You have a stolen something?

DERODA: Yes.

RAY: What do you call someone who steals?

DERODA: A robber.

RAY: A thief.

DERODA: Thief.

RAY: So what are you?

DERODA: Still a good person.

RAY: No, what are you if you steal?

DERODA: [Pauses]

RAY: A thief.

DERODA: Thief.

It's essential that the lost look directly into the mirror. The child has had her hand in the cookie jar and has chocolate all over her face. But she maintains her innocence. So her mom holds the mirror up to her guilty face and asks her what she sees. The mom wants to hear "Chocolate. I had my hand in the jar." Scripture says, "He who covers his sins will not prosper, but whoever confesses and forsakes them will have mercy" (Proverbs 28:13).

Asking "What are you called if you steal?" was to make Deroda face the truth. The apostle Paul was essentially saying this when he asked, "You who preach that a man should not steal, do you steal? You who say, 'Do not commit adultery,' do you commit adultery?" (Romans 2:21–22).

RAY: Have you ever used God's name in vain?

DERODA: Yes.

RAY: Would you use your mother's name as a cuss word?

DERODA: Probably not. No.

RAY: Of course not. That would dishonor her. If you want to express disgust—hit your thumb with a hammer and want to say [a cuss] word— you wouldn't substitute her name in its place. That would be a horrible thing to do. And yet you've done that with the name of God—the God who gave you life—when his name is holy. It's called blasphemy. It's so serious it's punishable by death in the Old Testament. I appreciate your patience with me. This is very awkward for you and for me.

DERODA: That's okay.

My appreciation of her patience was an oasis in the desert for her and me. This was hot going, and this was a slight pause to cool down for a moment. It let Deroda know that I cared about her and that I was aware that this was like being in a dentist chair. As a child, I sure appreciated hearing my dentist say that we were almost done.

RAY: You can handle it?

DERODA: I honestly…I really enjoy that people still talk about God and have such a strong faith and come out here and talk about it.

RAY: Oh, that's great. You've made me feel more relaxed. So here we go. We're bringing the cannons out now. Jesus said that if you look with lust, you commit adultery in your heart [see Matthew 5:28]. Have you ever looked with lust?

DERODA: [Laughs] Absolutely.

RAY: Have you had sex before marriage?

DERODA: Of course.

RAY: So…

DERODA: So, I'm not going to heaven. It sounds like that heaven just doesn't want me, and that's a real big shame that because I had sex before marriage that my chances of getting into heaven are limited, and I think that's a really crazy way to look at how God looks at us because, overall, you should be judged by your life on this earth, not because I told a lie and I took God's name or I had sex before marriage. There's so much more that goes into your life and what you should be judged on, and if that's the way heaven's going to judge, then I don't really need to go there.

I just stood in front of a Gatling gun of justification. Chocolate everywhere, and instead of saying, "I'm guilty. Please forgive me," the child railed at the mother that her guilt wasn't serious. I, therefore, wanted to address these points without sounding argumentative. So I tossed in a slight compliment by telling her that what she had just said was interesting. I was sincere with this, and by saying that, I wanted her to give me permission to respond unhindered.

RAY: That had a whole stack of stuff that's really interesting.

DERODA: I know.

RAY: So let me let me address the first one, and I think it's the basis of everything. Do you know what the first of the Ten Commandments is?

DERODA: Oh my gosh. Yes, I do. You will not have other gods before me.

RAY: Yes, it is. You nailed it. And that means don't make up a god in your own image. A god that has no sense of justice or righteousness or truth. I did before I was a Christian. I had a god that I snuggled up to and used to pray to every night, but he was a figment of my imagination. The place of imagery. I had an image of God that was erroneous, and from there I said, "Well, God doesn't care about right or wrong or fornication or blasphemy or lying or stealing." But we do. We'll chase a man to the end of the earth if he's violated the law—if he's seriously done something wrong. That's because we're made in God's image. The God of the Bible does care about right and wrong, and so back to the question.

On judgment day, you're a self-admitted lying, thieving, blasphemous, fornicating adulterer at heart, will you be innocent or guilty if he judges you by the Ten Commandments?

DERODA: Totally guilty.

RAY: Heaven or hell?

DERODA: I'm going to hell.

RAY: Now, does that concern you?

DERODA: You know, it used to when I was younger, and as I got older and like really just sat with myself and was able to make my own choices about God, I learned that I don't have to do everything that the Ten Commandments say. I grew up super religious, and I question my parents now, too, and hearing a lot of the things that my parents follow and how close-minded they are, it really just pushes me further away.

RAY: Well, Deroda,…if you could be patient with me. It horrifies me, the thought of you ending up in hell. I've just met you, but I care about you, and the thought of you ending up in hell breaks my heart. Now, do you know what the Bible says death actually is?

DERODA: I don't.

RAY: It says death is wages. Did you know that?

DERODA: Is what?

RAY: Wages.

DERODA: Wages?

RAY: Yes. God is paying you in death for your sins. It's like a judge in the court of law sees a heinous criminal who's murdered three young ladies. He says, "We're going to pay you in the death sentence. This is your wages. This is what's due to you. This is what you've earned." We think lightly of sin. Who doesn't lie and steal and fornicate and all that? But God says because he's holy, that sin is so serious, he's given you capital punishment. Death is evidence that God is serious about sin.

It had been quite some time since Deroda dismissed Scripture as being unreliable, saying that it had changed through the ages, mentioning the ever-popular phone game analogy. I had decided not to address her issues with the Bible at that point because she needed to hear the gospel. My agenda is never to argue about the inspiration of the Bible. I wanted to wait to see if she had a humble heart. And she proved to have just that. So I decided then to address the subject.

RAY: And you said before, "The Bible has changed." I've been reading it every day without fail for about forty-eight years, and I've never found a mistake in it. I can go back to the original Greek and Hebrew. There are no changes. They've been very diligent. And this whole phone conversation—that phone game? That's okay if the person who sent the message follows the phone all the way through, so it doesn't change, and that's what God has done with this Word. He's honored his Word. He's kept his Word. It hasn't changed.

So, tell me, you were brought up a Catholic, so see if you know what God did for guilty sinners so we wouldn't have to go to hell. Do you know?

DERODA: He died.

RAY: He suffered and died on the cross. Now most people know that, but it doesn't mean much to them because they don't understand one important thought. Let me share it with you and get your thoughts.

"And get your thoughts" is an important phrase I often use. It tells the person that I am not going to lecture them or preach at them. They are going to get a chance to share their thoughts. That helps to momentarily quell any objections they may have so that I can present the gospel without any interruptions that may distract from its purity.

RAY: The Ten Commandments are called the moral law. You and I broke the law, and Jesus paid the fine. That's what happened on that cross. That's why he said, "It is finished," just before he died [John 19:30]. Deroda, that's a weird thing to say before you die, "It is finished," but he was saying that the debt has been paid. We broke God's law; Jesus paid the fine.

If you're in court and someone pays your fine, a judge can legally let you go. He can say, "Look, there's a stack of speeding fines here. It's serious, but someone's paid them; you're out of here." And he can do that which is legal. And God can *legally* dismiss your case, take the death sentence off you, let you walk, guilty though you are, and grant you everlasting life as a free gift—not because you're good but because he's good, rich in mercy, and he provided a Savior who paid our fine.

And then, Jesus rose from the dead and defeated death, and if you'll simply repent of your sins…Go straight to God and say, "I've done things I know are abhorrent to you that are worthy of the death sentence; I ask you to forgive me, cleanse me." That's genuine repentance. And then trust in Jesus like you trust a parachute. If you're on a plane ten thousand feet up and you didn't put a parachute on, you're going to perish. But the parachute will be put on because you know you're in danger. That's why people put parachutes on—because they know they're going to hit the ground at 120 miles an hour.

What I've tried to do with you today is put the fear of God in you because I know the fear of God is the beginning of wisdom, and fear in that sense, that makes you put on a parachute, is actually good. It's doing you a favor. Fear in this sense, realizing your salvation is at stake, will cause you to get right with God and say, "I have sinned against you."…Everlasting life is a free gift of God. You've been so patient with me. Here's me rattling on, and you didn't butt in, but you listened, and I really appreciate that. You're going to think about what we talked about?

DERODA: I always do. I always like to listen and take it all in because you can only become a wiser and stronger person if you listen to others, others who do the research and others who read the Bible down the line, so I appreciate your time too.

RAY: I'm honored that you have listened…and you're going to think about it seriously?

DERODA: Let's rock and roll, yes.

RAY: Yes, you know why I say the word *seriously*? It's because you don't know when you're going to die. It could be tonight in your sleep, could be on the way home. One hundred fifty thousand people die every twenty-four hours, so think about it and think about the words of Jesus: "What should it profit a man (and that means a woman too) if he shall gain the whole world and lose his own soul?" [Matthew 16:26, author's paraphrase]. Your life is so precious, and so think about it with that sense of urgency. I'd like to give you a book that I've written. Is that okay?

DERODA: Sure, thanks.

RAY: [Gives her *How to Be Free from the Fear of Death*] Do you think you'll read it?

DERODA: Cool. I will read it…I appreciate that you feel so strongly about your belief, and you want to come out here, and you want to let everybody know. So, thanks for being here.

What a joy it is to speak with someone who has an open and humble heart. When I first began speaking with her and heard her condone illegal drug usage, I wondered where the conversation would go. But it shouldn't be surprising Deroda sought her own version of heaven. Many do. The confidence that humans can find a pleasurable eternal life on their own is only possible when they ignore the deadly ramifications of their sin and refuse to see God for who he truly is: more just, holy, and merciful than any godlike idol they could conjure.

Yet after seeing her sin, Deroda was willing to admit her guilt and need for a Savior. I was delighted with her response.

CHAPTER 7

A MIX OF BELIEFS

Many of us advertise our beliefs by how we dress. Of course, this isn't always the case, but it certainly was with Catherine. One look at the occultic symbolism she wore, especially the trinket around her neck, and I suspected that I was going to be dealing directly with demons. My suspicions proved to be true as I began hearing her strange and sometimes double-minded answers that came from mixing the occult with religion and other beliefs. But under the confusion was a young woman who was desperately searching for truth in the wrong places. I was praying that God would give me wisdom so that I could show her the answer to the *Why Jesus?* question.

RAY: Do you believe God exists?

CATHERINE: Yes, I do, sir.

RAY: Who was Jesus?

CATHERINE: Geronimo.

RAY: Jesus of the Bible, I'm talking about.

CATHERINE: Jesus of Nazareth.

Catherine believed in God's existence, but she still had a very real battle within her mind. That is nothing out of the ordinary. The mind is the place of spiritual attacks as well as the place of strongholds (see 2 Corinthians 10:4–5). The Scriptures tell us that we're enemies of God *in our mind* through wicked works (see Colossians 1:21). The Bible speaks of the *mind* of the flesh (see Romans 8:6).

I decided to cut to the chase and ask if she thought Jesus was the Christ, the Son of the living God. This was based on 1 John 4:1–3: "Beloved, do not believe every spirit, but test the spirits, whether they are of God; because many false prophets have gone out into the world. By this you know the Spirit of God: Every spirit that confesses that Jesus Christ has come in the flesh is of God, and every spirit that does not confess that Jesus Christ has come in the flesh is not of God. And this is the spirit of the Antichrist, which you have heard was coming, and is now already in the world." The world is full of lies, and Christians need to discern what is of God and what isn't.

RAY: Yes. Do you know what he did for humanity?

CATHERINE: Yes, he saved us all.

Jesus didn't save us all. He said, "Enter by the narrow gate; for wide is the gate and broad is the way that leads to destruction, and there are many who go in by it. Because narrow is the gate and difficult is the way which leads to life, and there are few who find it" (Matthew 7:13–14).

To believe that Jesus has saved everybody isn't based on the Scriptures but rather rooted in idolatry. This belief means that all is now well between humanity and God and that he doesn't command sinners to repent. Neither is there a need to trust in Jesus for personal salvation. It's like believing that because parachutes exist, no one needs to put their trust in one. They can jump without it and not suffer the consequences. This is what the Scriptures call "another gospel."

Look at the apostle Paul's sobering warning about preaching anything other than the biblical gospel: "I marvel that you are turning away so soon from Him who called you in the grace of Christ, to a different gospel, which is not another; but there are some who trouble you and want to pervert the gospel of Christ. But even if we, or an angel from heaven, preach any other gospel to you than what we have preached to you, let him be accursed. As we have said before, so now I say again, if anyone preaches any other gospel to you than what you have received, let him be accursed" (Galatians 1:6–9).

> RAY: Well, he made *provision* for us to have everlasting life.
>
> CATHERINE: Yes, he did.
>
> RAY: Yes.
>
> CATHERINE: I'm a Catholic.
>
> RAY: Have you been born again?
>
> CATHERINE: I was saved my whole life. I was christened. I've never stopped being a Catholic. All I did was open up my mind to other religions, and I learned that all religions have truth.
>
> RAY: You said you're a Catholic and that you've been saved all your life.
>
> CATHERINE: Yes.
>
> RAY: The Bible says to be born again, and Jesus said unless you're born again, you'll not enter into the kingdom of heaven [see John 3:3].
>
> CATHERINE: Then I must have been born again because then I remembered who I was by God's grace, and I was saved by Saint Christopher, so I believe.

Her comment about Saint Christopher was a rabbit trail I didn't want to go down to avoid causing

Catherine to become defensive before I began to share the truth of the gospel.

> CATHERINE: I went to any church I could, and I gave my soul to God, and I prayed and I prayed and I prayed, and I said I know I'm a martyr, but I won't allow myself to be killed again for my cause. Our Father, who art in heaven, hallowed be thy name. Forgive us our trespasses as we forgive those who trespassed against us…

This was becoming weird. I was surprised when she randomly launched into the Lord's Prayer during a normal conversation. A psychologist would no doubt have a diagnosis for her rambling, but it was clear that the *source* was spiritual. Some may question why I didn't cast out the demon there and then. This is because of what the Scriptures tell us: "When an unclean spirit goes out of a man, he goes through dry places, seeking rest, and finds none. Then he says, 'I will return to my house from which I came.' And when he comes, he finds it empty, swept, and put in order. Then he goes and takes with him seven other spirits more wicked than himself, and they enter and dwell there; and the last state of that man is worse than the first. So shall it also be with this wicked generation" (Matthew 12:43–45).

If Catherine didn't truly repent, it would leave the door open for her to become much worse. She needed to turn from all sin and be born again through faith in Jesus. That means submitting to God. Then, when she resists the devil, he would flee from her. As James says, "Adulterers and adulteresses! Do you not know that friendship with the world is enmity with God? Whoever therefore wants to be a friend of the world makes himself an enemy of God. Or do you think that the Scripture says in vain, 'The Spirit who dwells in us yearns jealously'? But He gives more grace. Therefore He says: 'God resists the proud, but gives grace to the humble.' Therefore submit to God. Resist the devil and he will flee from you" (4:4–7).

This is why I then drew her attention to the occult trinket she was wearing around her neck.

RAY: I can't help but notice something around your neck. What is that?

CATHERINE: This is a collar, and it's one that I'm going to be removing in front of everyone.

RAY: It's demonic, isn't it? Isn't it the occult?

CATHERINE: It's Wiccan. I'm a Wiccan, and I don't believe in Satan. I believe in demons though. I've seen demons.

Based on what I'd already heard and seen, I wasn't surprised to hear her acknowledge her occultic involvement.

> Wicca, a predominantly Western movement whose followers practice witchcraft and nature worship and who see it as a religion based on pre-Christian traditions of northern and western Europe. It spread through England in the 1950s and subsequently attracted followers in Europe and the United States.
>
> Although there were precursors to the movement, the origins of modern Wicca can be traced to a retired British civil servant, Gerald Brousseau Gardner (1884–1964). Gardner spent most of his career in Asia, where he became familiar with a variety of occult beliefs and magical practices. He also read widely in Western esoteric literature, including the writings of the British occultist Aleister Crowley.[7]

Being informed about different worldviews and beliefs can help us evangelize even if we don't directly address how these beliefs oppose what Scripture says. Staying informed helps us understand people's current perspectives and beliefs and use this knowledge to speak to them more personally.

RAY: So, have you been speaking to the dead?

CATHERINE: Yes, because they walk again like Jesus said they would, like Lazarus.

RAY: But the Bible says don't speak with the dead because they're familiar spirits and they'll deceive you.

CATHERINE: They did. I didn't listen. I should have.

The word *familiar*, derived from the Latin *familiaris*, means a "household servant." This definition conveys the idea that spirits served their masters and obeyed their commands. Even people who try to contact the dead in modern times say they communicate with and are guided by familiar spirits.[8] A medium is one who acts as a liaison to supposedly contact or communicate with the dead on behalf of the living. In reality, mediums are contacting demons who convince the mediums that they are "familiar" and can be trusted and believed.

God banned the practices associated with mediums and familiar spirits in Israel because they are an abomination to the Lord, and the punishment for getting involved with spirits and mediums was death.[9]

When you come into the land which the LORD your God is giving you, you shall not learn to follow the abominations of those nations. There shall not be found among you anyone who makes his son or his daughter pass through the fire, or one who practices witchcraft, or a soothsayer, or one who interprets omens, or a sorcerer, or one who conjures spells, or a medium, or a spiritist, or one who calls up the dead. For all who do these things are an abomination to the LORD, and because of these abominations the LORD your God drives them out from before you. (Deuteronomy 18:9–12)

When we are witnessing to people who say they hold beliefs that don't align with Scripture, we ask ourselves if we should try to untangle the web of unbiblical beliefs. While I will warn people of the dangers of harmful practices, like I did with Catherine, I rarely attempt to explain why their beliefs are untrue because it may spark needless contention that puts the person I'm trying to reach on the defensive. I don't want that. I want them to be open to my reasoning.

So instead, I want to center that reasoning on righteousness, self-control, and judgment. This is what the apostle Paul did with Felix, governor of Judea: "After some days, when Felix came with his wife Drusilla, who was Jewish, he sent for Paul and heard him concerning the faith in Christ. Now as he reasoned about righteousness, self-control, and the judgment to come, Felix was afraid and answered, 'Go away for now; when I have a convenient time I will call for you'" (Acts 24:24–25).

Felix was afraid, for good reason, because Paul put the fear of God in him. The Scriptures say, "The fear of the LORD is a fountain of life, to turn one away from the snares of death" (Proverbs 14:27).

His sin was an offense to God. To get to that place with Catherine, I needed to keep the focus on getting to the gospel. The Scriptures tell us that the gospel "is the power of God to salvation" (Romans 1:16). In other words, the gospel is the means by which a sinner's understanding is opened and his or her soul saved.

To address the theological errors of the ungodly at this point is to tend to the symptoms of a disease while ignoring the cause. Anyone who genuinely experiences the new birth of John 3 will then read and believe the Scriptures, and when they see the many discrepancies between the Word of God and their man-made beliefs, they will have to make a decision. Do they stay with the errors instilled by human thoughts and practices or follow the truth of the Word of God? The benefit of addressing the root cause of Catherine's separation from God—her sin nature—will be that any conviction to keep or abandon her current beliefs will come from her personal desire to please God, rather than by me coercing her.

RAY: Now, are you a good person?

CATHERINE: I am.

RAY: Do you know that Bible says none are good [see Psalm 14:1], and the reason we say we're good is because we compare ourselves to our standards rather than God's.

CATHERINE: I want to be like an angel.

RAY: Well, let's see if you're a good person…if you're going to make it to heaven. I'm going to give you a moral standard to judge yourself by, the Ten Commandments. So, let's go through a few of them and see how you're going to do on judgment day.

CATHERINE: All right, I'm not going to do too well, but God will forgive me.

RAY: Can you be honest with me?

CATHERINE: Yes, sir.

RAY: How many lies have you told in your life?

CATHERINE: Many, to protect the truth.

RAY: Have you ever stolen something?

CATHERINE: No.

RAY: Have you used God's name in vain?

CATHERINE: I have, and I apologized, and God said he forgave me.

RAY: It's blasphemy when you do that. It's very serious.

CATHERINE: I know, and I'm sorry, but guess what? God's forgiveness is infinite.

Once again, here was a rabbit trail of unsound doctrine. When you take someone through the commandments, never forget that your battle isn't against flesh and blood but against spiritual wickedness in high places (see Ephesians 6:12–20), so be on your guard for distractions that will take you away from your agenda. While there are many verses in Scripture about God's mercy enduring forever, we can't rest our salvation on a presumption that God will always forgive. Ask the Noah generation or ask Sodom and Gomorrah if God's forgiveness is infinite. As they found out, the time comes when God loses patience and judgment comes.

There are times when we will feel free to correct error. Jesus spoke to the woman at the well about her violation of the seventh commandment *and* answered her questions about where to get living water and where people should worship. Notice her subtle denial of adultery and how Jesus came back on point:

> Jesus said to her, "Go, call your husband, and come here."
>
> The woman answered and said, "I have no husband."

Jesus said to her, "You have well said, 'I have no husband,' for you have had five husbands, and the one whom you now have is not your husband; in that you spoke truly."

The woman said to Him, "Sir, I perceive that You are a prophet. Our fathers worshiped on this mountain, and you Jews say that in Jerusalem is the place where one ought to worship."

Jesus said to her, "Woman, believe Me, the hour is coming when you will neither on this mountain, nor in Jerusalem, worship the Father. You worship what you do not know; we know what we worship, for salvation is of the Jews. But the hour is coming, and now is, when the true worshipers will worship the Father in spirit and truth; for the Father is seeking such to worship Him. God is Spirit, and those who worship Him must worship in spirit and truth." (John 4:16–24)

Jesus addressed her question *after* he had addressed her sin.

RAY: Jesus said that if you look with lust, you commit adultery in your heart [see Matthew 5:28]. Have you ever looked with lust?

CATHERINE: No, I haven't. I've always been a faithful woman.

RAY: Have you had sex before marriage?

CATHERINE: Yes, I have, but it wasn't by choice.

RAY: You were raped?

CATHERINE: My whole life…Pressured into sex so bad I'm trying to get [expletive] out of here. Excuse my language.

RAY: So, what I'm trying to do with you is show you sin in its true light so you can be genuinely sorry before God because…

CATHERINE: I am very repentant, of course. But of course, God's issues and commands are different for saints than they are for people.

RAY: No, the Bible says…

CATHERINE: The Bible was edited by William Shakespeare. I'm a new age Christian. I read the Gnostic books. I read the Dead Sea Scrolls. I read every book I could. You want to know why? I wanted to know the truth.

Again, these were more rabbit trails to be ignored—Shakespeare writing the Bible, the fallacies of the new age movement, and the Gnostic gospels.

The Gnostics fraudulently attached the names of famous Christians to their writings, such as the gospel of Thomas, the gospel of Philip, the gospel of Mary, etc. The discovery of the Nag Hammadi library in southern Egypt in 1945 represented a major discovery of Gnostic gospels. These Gnostic gospels are often pointed to as supposed "lost books of the Bible."

So, what are we to make of the Gnostic gospels? Should some or all of them be in the Bible? No, they should not. First, as pointed out above, the Gnostic gospels are forgeries, fraudulently written in the names of the Apostles in order to give them a legitimacy in the early church.[10]

While it is important for us as Christians to understand different worldviews, opinions, and objection people may have, tackling each erroneous statement distracts from our main purpose: to show people why Jesus is the only path to salvation.

RAY: I care about you. I want to see you in heaven, not in hell. So, you need to truly repent and put your faith in Jesus. Can I pray for you?

CATHERINE: Of course you can.

RAY: Tell me your name again?

CATHERINE: Lady Catherine of Aragon. I'm a sister. I'm a nun.

RAY: Okay. Father, I pray for Catherine. I...pray that you'll speak to her heart, and today may she understand the love that you have for her soul. May she truly repent, be born again, and pass from death to life because of your mercy. In Jesus' name we pray, amen.

CATHERINE: Amen.

It's always a challenge sharing the gospel with someone when you know there is serious demonic activity. The thought enters my mind as to how much this person is being influenced by demons. However, my consolation is the case of Legion. Even though that man was terribly demon possessed, those demonic forces couldn't stop him from coming to Jesus: "When He stepped out on the land, there met Him a certain man from the city who had demons for a long time. And he wore no clothes, nor did he live in a house but in the tombs. When he saw Jesus, he cried out, fell down before Him, and with a loud voice said, 'What have I to do with You, Jesus, Son of the Most High God? I beg You, do not torment me!'" (Luke 8:27–28). May we be encouraged that Jesus saves even those with the darkest pasts if they come to him with a repentant heart.

CHAPTER 8

THE DANGERS OF SIN

I was driving on a major freeway in Los Angeles when I saw a man actually standing on the busy freeway (about one hundred feet in front of me). My first thought was that he was an absolute fool because he could have been killed by the speeding traffic. But I then saw what he was doing. He had parked his van in the carpool lane and was pulling a large mattress off the freeway, obviously concerned about the traffic hitting the mattress. To run over an empty cardboard box at seventy miles an hour is frightening even though it would likely be crushed under the wheel. However, suddenly running into a mattress at that speed could be fatal. This man wasn't a fool. He was a hero.

We Christians know that the world is in great danger. That's why we make ourselves look like fools to warn others. Love and concern cannot remain passive. They are the fountain of our evangelism. Think of what Jesus did. He humbled himself and became obedient to death. He was stripped and humiliated by this evil world—all for our redemption. If he would do that for us, we should be able to suffer a little humiliation for him.

One of the biggest hindrances to the gospel, if not *the* biggest hindrance, is human pride. Especially among today's youth. But I have found a gentle and subtle way to humble a person without them realizing it right at the beginning of an interview.

I ask, "Are you an educated person? Are you well-read?" Most tell me that they certainly are. Then I ask if they know the world's best-selling book of all time. Most don't. I tell them that it is the Bible and ask, "Have you ever read the Bible?" Most haven't. It is the best-selling book of all time, and they haven't even opened it. That gives me an upper hand for what I say next. I ask, "Have you heard the famous Bible verse (and I then quote the verse I want to share)?" So I now have a humbled sinner listening intently to what I have to share rather than someone with a proud heart refusing to engage.

One day, a tall, handsome man in his early twenties named Johnny shocked and humbled *me*. He knew that the Bible was the world's best-selling book of all time, and he was familiar with the Bible verse I mentioned. I was both delighted and surprised.

RAY: What's the biggest-selling book of all time?

JOHNNY: I would think it would be the Bible.

RAY: Right! Are you familiar with the Bible verse, "The Son of Man has come to seek and save that which is lost" [Luke 19:10, author's paraphrase]?

JOHNNY: I went to a Christian school.

RAY: Are you lost?

JOHNNY: Sometimes. I believe I am. Yes.

RAY: So, the Son of Man has come to seek and to save you?

JOHNNY: That might be true…yes.

RAY: Do you think you're a good person?

JOHNNY: I'd like to say so, yes.

RAY: My problem is that I believe you're in great danger, but you don't realize it. Do you believe you're in great danger?

JOHNNY: No, not right now.

So many people who think they're good not only affirm the rightness of the Bible and the Ten Commandments, but they wrongly think that they can find comfort in them. Let's now look at Romans 7:7–13

from the *Amplified Bible*. Listen to the apostle Paul
speak of the law's influence on his conversion to Christ:

> What shall we say then? Is the Law sin?
> Certainly not! On the contrary, if it had not been
> for the Law, I would not have recognized sin.
> For I would not have known [for example] about
> coveting [what belongs to another, and would
> have had no sense of guilt] if the Law had not
> [repeatedly] said, "You shall not covet." But sin,
> finding an opportunity through the command-
> ment [to express itself] produced in me every
> kind of coveting and selfish desire. (vv. 7–8)

Sin is like a mighty river, pushing against the
cracked dam of our will. It is overpowering, and yet
without the law, there is no recognition of its destruc-
tive power. It's just the way it is. The water cracks the
dam; the moth goes to the burning flame. But watch
how the law brings understanding as to its dreadful
consequences:

> For without the Law sin is dead [the rec-
> ognition of sin is inactive]. I was once alive
> without [knowledge of] the Law; but when the
> commandment came [and I understood its
> meaning], sin became alive and I died [since
> the Law sentenced me to death]. And the very

commandment which was intended to bring life, actually proved to bring death for me. (vv. 8–10)

So when I begin to take Johnny through the commandments, he's not going to find comfort but condemnation. The law will bring death, not life. He will be looking for hope, but each one of the commandments proves to be an enemy, not a friend. The law is going to kill false hope and leave him helpless and hopeless. That will kill any supposed refuge in self-righteousness and make him look for mercy.

> For sin, seizing its opportunity through the commandment, beguiled and completely deceived me, and using it as a weapon killed me [separating me from God]. So then, the Law is holy, and the commandment is holy and righteous and good.
>
> Did that which is good [the Law], then become death to me? Certainly not! But sin, in order that it might be revealed as sin, was producing death in me by [using] this good thing [as a weapon], so that through the commandment sin would become exceedingly sinful. (vv. 11–13)

The results of sin have caused an ocean of tears. It is a deadly poison that destroys every victim. And yet the truth of this danger hides from us until the law gives us light.

RAY: Can you be honest with me?

JOHNNY: Sure.

RAY: How many lies have you told in your life? Quite a few?

JOHNNY: Yes.

RAY: I'm going to take you through the Ten Commandments to show you're in danger. So what do you call someone who tells lies?

JOHNNY: A liar.

RAY: So, do you still think you're a good person?

JOHNNY: Yes.

RAY: Have you ever stolen something?

JOHNNY: When I was a kid, I probably stole a few things, yes.

RAY: So, what do you call someone who steals?

JOHNNY: A thief.

RAY: So, what are you?

JOHNNY: I guess I'd be a thief.

RAY: No, you're not, you're a lying thief.

JOHNNY: [Laughs] Yes, I'm a lying thief.

RAY: Now, do you still think you're a good person?

JOHNNY: Yes, I do.

RAY: Have you ever used God's name in vain?

JOHNNY: Yes.

RAY: Do you love your mum?

JOHNNY: Of course I do.

RAY: Would you ever use her name as a cuss word? You hit your thumb with a hammer, you could say [a cuss word]. Would you substitute her name in the place of that filth word to express disgust?

JOHNNY: Probably not. I don't think it would be as satisfying.

Here is something important. Johnny admitted something we don't hear too often: blasphemy is far more satisfying to spit out than an ordinary cuss word.

As you may have noticed, almost all those I interview admit they have used God's name in vain. In a book I wrote called *Hallowed Be Thy Name*, I looked closely at how often people in Hollywood blaspheme the names of Jesus and God. Interestingly, people said that when wanting to express something absolutely disgusting, using God's name and the name of Jesus worked perfectly. That certainly confirms that the human mind is at enmity against God and that it hates him without cause. Oh, how evil we are! Our wonderful

Creator gave us the gift of life and lavishes his kindness upon us, and we spit in his face.

The Bible says this of Jesus: "For even Christ did not please Himself; but as it is written, 'The reproaches of those who reproached You fell on Me'" (Romans 15:3). In other words, all the hatred that humans had for God became unified into one clenched and violent fist that smashed in wrath against the sinless Lamb of God.

> RAY: It wouldn't be as satisfying as using God's name in its place, and that's what you've done. You've taken the holy name of God that godly Jews won't even speak because it's so holy, and you've substituted for that [cuss] word—and he's the one who gave you your mother. He gave you your eyesight, your hearing, your brain, your taste buds, the ability to enjoy good music. He's lavished his kindness upon you, and you've taken his name and used it in that way. Do you know what that's called?
>
> JOHNNY: Is that blasphemy?
>
> RAY: Blasphemy—punishable by death in the Old Testament. Do you still think you're a good person?
>
> JOHNNY: I still do.

I so thank God for his law. Without it, we would be powerless when it comes dealing with the stubborn root of self-righteousness. Without it, we would be unable to express our need for repentance or for a Savior.

RAY: Jesus said, "Whoever looks at a woman and lusts for her has committed adultery already with her in his heart" [Matthew 5:28, author paraphrase]. Have you ever looked at a woman with lust?

JOHNNY: Of course I have.

RAY: Have you had sex before marriage?

JOHNNY: Yes.

RAY: Do you know what causes death?

JOHNNY: No.

RAY: Death is wages. "The wages of sin is death" [Romans 6:23]. Ever heard that?

JOHNNY: Yes, I have.

RAY: Death is what God pays you for your sins. It's like a judge in a court of law has a heinous criminal who has murdered three girls after he raped them. And the judge says, "You've *earned* the death sentence. This is your *wages*. This is what's *due* to you. This is your *payment*." And sin is so serious to a holy God...not to us (who doesn't lie? Who doesn't steal? Who doesn't blaspheme? Who doesn't lust or fornicate?), but it's so serious to God that he's given you capital punishment for your sins.

So here's that summation. I'm not judging you, but you've told me you're a lying, thieving, fornicating, blasphemous adulterer at heart who is self-righteous, that is, you say you're a good person when it's obvious you're not—you're like the rest of us. So, can you see you've earned your wages?

JOHNNY: I still think I'm a good person.

RAY: You're going to hang on to that?

JOHNNY: Yes.

Self-righteousness will arguably take more people to hell than any other sin. Have you ever noticed how stubborn weeds are? They grow through cracks in concrete. They grow up on the sides of freeways where there is no soil or regular water. And so it is with the curse of self-righteousness. It grows up like a stubborn weed in the human heart. You think you've dealt with it, and back it comes, hindering a blind and proud sinner from seeing the glorious light of the gospel. I can only pray that continuing to see his sin against the light of the law will reveal to Johnny how far he is from God.

RAY: You think a lying thief is a good person? When did you last look at pornography?

JOHNNY: This morning.

Johnny was being honest. His house was on fire, and he was awake to it, but he wasn't alarmed. So then I needed to do everything I could to alarm him. I wanted him to smell the smoke, see the flames, and run from the house. If he wouldn't run, I'd pull him out of his complacency. "On some have compassion, making a distinction; but others save with fear, *pulling them out of the fire*, hating even the garment defiled by the flesh" (Jude 1:22–23, emphasis added).

RAY: Can you see that there's a standard that you've got of righteousness and the standard of God's righteousness? God's morally perfect. When he says "good," he means morally perfect in thought, word, and deed. If you hate someone, the Bible says you're a murderer [see 1 John 3:15]. That's how high God's standard is. Your problem is that you don't see your danger, and I do. If you died today and God gave you justice…you're playing a bit of basketball, if your heart gave out, they'd say, "Man, he died young…didn't realize he had a weak heart. No one knew. He looked healthy." You're in eternity, and God will damn you—he'll give you justice—and the Bible says, "All liars will have their part in the lake of fire" [Revelation 21:8, author's paraphrase].

My ally is your conscience. That is, God's given you a conscience that's independent of your will. When you do something morally wrong, it accuses you. When you lie, it says, "That was wrong." You can deny the voice of conscience if you wish, but that's like taking the batteries out of your smoke detector. So that keeps going off and annoying you—sounding the alarm—so you take it out. It's there for your good. I'm hoping your conscience is doing its duty and saying, "Man, you're in big trouble with your Creator." If you want to live forever, if you don't want to be damned, you better obey the gospel. Have you ever heard the gospel?

JOHNNY: Yes.

RAY: You have?

JOHNNY: Yes, I mean, I grew up going to church and everything.

Those who grew up in the church and heard the gospel but still live in sin more than likely never understood it. Otherwise they would be saved. To understand it means to understand your moral state and therefore your great danger, a danger you cannot save yourself from. Or perhaps Johnny had heard the modern gospel that is so prevalent within the contemporary church, where Jesus is preached as the great problem solver, the one who gives true and lasting happiness. Such a "gospel" is irrelevant to those who are enjoying the pleasures of sin for a season. So, I called Johnny's bluff to see if he had heard the biblical gospel.

> RAY: Okay, explain it to me.
>
> JOHNNY: Well, I wouldn't be able to explain it to you.
>
> RAY: Let me give you my take on it, and it might click, you never know.

This phrase "Let me give you my take on it, and it might click, you never know" takes away any thought that I am preaching down to people. I don't want to sound superior or condescending, but rather, I want people like Johnny to see that I'm a friend who is coming alongside them, giving them another perspective.

> RAY: There's something in you that says, "Oh, I don't want to die." When you said you weren't afraid of dying, I knew you weren't telling the truth because the Bible says *every* human being is haunted by the fear of death all their lifetime [see Hebrews 2:15]. God has placed eternity on their hearts. There's something in us that says

life is precious; I want to hold on to it; and Jesus said, "If you seek to save your life, you're going to lose it" [Luke 17:33, author's paraphrase].

So, here's the gospel, and it may give you a different perspective that you can hang on to. Most people know that Christ died for our sins, but they don't know this…the Ten Commandments (that which we've just looked at) are called the moral law. You and I broke the law. Jesus paid the fine. Do you remember his last words on the cross just before he dismissed his Spirit? He said three very profound words. He said, "It is finished" [John 19:30]. It is finished. Why did he say that? It's a strange thing to say when you're dying, but he was saying that the debt has been paid. You and I broke the law. Jesus paid the fine.

John, if you're in court and someone pays your speeding fines, the judge can let you go. He can say, "There's a stack of spending fines; it's very serious, but someone's paid them—you're out of here." And he can do that which is legal, right, and just. And God can legally dismiss your case. He can let you live forever. He can take the death sentence off you, all because Jesus paid the fine in his life's blood. He evened the scales. That's what that death was about. That's why he came—so that you could find everlasting life and not be subject to death. You've got death written all over you, you know, until you come to Christ. Then Jesus rose from the dead; it was impossible for death to hold him, the Bible says [see Acts 2:24].

If you'll simply repent of your sins, let go of them and say, "God, I've been doing things I know are morally wrong. I've been feasting on unclean things, pornography, and having sex out of marriage, and lying, and stealing, and blaspheming your name. I'm so sorry." The way to find sorrow is to look at what it cost God for your forgiveness; he became a human being, suffered, and died on that cross. The wrath of God came upon him so it wouldn't have to come upon you. And if you repent and trust in him, God promises he'll remit your sins in an instant and give you a new heart with new desires. That's the personal miracle that God will give you so that you love righteousness, so that you won't do that which is wrong. You *want* to do that which is right.

Do you remember the first and greatest commandment? You shall love the Lord your God with all your heart, mind, soul, and strength. That's what God requires of you.

You're like the rest of us. You've gone astray, and you've loved sin and walked with your back to the God who gave you life. If you'll turn to him, he'll give you a clean heart that loves righteousness and grant everlasting life as a free gift. Do you think I'm telling the truth?

JOHNNY: Yes, of course.

What an encouragement those words were from Johnny! I had just run a verbal marathon, and he was telling me that it was worth all my effort. But even if he had said that I had wasted my time, I would fall back on this promise of God: "Therefore, my beloved brethren, be steadfast, immovable, always abounding in the work of the Lord, knowing that your labor is not in vain in the Lord" (1 Corinthians 15:58).

However, I would be cheating you to give you a verse that begins with *therefore* without reading the preceding wonderful verses to give it context. Here they are:

Now this I say, brethren, that flesh and blood cannot inherit the kingdom of God; nor does corruption inherit incorruption. Behold, I tell you a mystery: We shall not all sleep, but we shall all be changed—in a moment, in the twinkling of an eye, at the last trumpet. For the trumpet will sound, and the dead will be raised incorruptible, and we shall be changed. For this corruptible must put on incorruption, and this mortal must put on immortality. So when this corruptible has put on incorruption, and this mortal has put on immortality, then shall be brought to pass the saying that is written: "Death is swallowed up in victory."

"O Death, where is your sting?

O Hades, where is your victory?"

The sting of death is sin, and the strength of sin is the law. But thanks be to God, who gives us the victory through our Lord Jesus Christ.

Therefore, my beloved brethren, be steadfast, immovable, always abounding in the work of the Lord, knowing that your labor is not in vain in the Lord. (vv. 50–58, emphasis added)

Why should we always be steadfast in our labor for the gospel? Why should we be stubbornly immovable, *always abounding* in that labor knowing that it's not in vain? Because we are laboring with Almighty God, who has accomplished through the gospel the most amazing, most wonderfully incredible thing for humanity. He destroyed death and brought life and immortality to light for dying sinners! How could we ever become discouraged? We will not. We cannot.

> RAY: I wouldn't lie to you. This is so important, and I'm so honored that you've listened to me. Are you going to think about what we talked about?

> JOHNNY: Yes, I mean, a conversation like this would always be impactful to anyone. I believe in signs, you know, miracles maybe. Something of a greater power coming to me…[Pause]

> RAY: Well, I prayed before I came to you. I didn't think anyone would be out today because it's so cold, and here you are. And I believe God's hand is upon you, and he doesn't want you to be subject to death. He doesn't want you to end up in hell. The Bible says that he has "no pleasure in the death of the wicked" [Ezekiel 33:11]. It's his will that all repent and come to Christ. So, are you going to get right with God? Are you going to repent and trust in Christ?

> JOHNNY: I mean it wouldn't be an easy thing of clicking a switch on and off, you know, I feel like…

Johnny's conscience had done its work, and he should be saying, "What must I do to be saved?" But he wasn't. He was lying in bed, seeing the smoke and the flames, but he wasn't appropriately alarmed. So next, I—with the help of God—tried my best to alarm him. And by the way, my "with the help of God" is not an empty maxim. When we open our mouths in faith— when we trust God to help us—he will. That's why I pray before every encounter, and the reason I pray is primarily because of six frightening words in Scripture: "Without Me you can do nothing" (John 15:5).

I don't want to do nothing.

I'm going to say something that is not false humility. I'm not clever, nor am I intelligent or eloquent. All you are reading in these transcripts is something I have done many times. So don't put me on a pedestal onto which I don't belong. Realize that you, too, will have an answer for everyone *if you trust the Lord*. He will give you the necessary wisdom as you step out in faith.

Here was my best shot with Johnny:

RAY: Well, let me see if I can make it clear what's going on. You're like a man on the edge of a plane ten thousand feet up. You know you have to jump, you don't have a parachute, and I say, "You're not going to put the parachute on?"

You say, "Well, that wouldn't be an easy thing to do."

JOHNNY: [Laughs] Well, yes, when you put it that way.

RAY: The best thing I could do for you in that instance would be to hang you out of the plane by your ankles for two seconds, and you'll come in and say, "Give me that parachute!" If you could just realize how terrifying it would be if you were to die in your sins, worse than falling out of a plane and hitting the ground 120 miles an hour. Death is horrific on this side, *but wait to get to the other side.* The Bible says that liars will have their part in the lake of fire; no thief, no blasphemer, no adulterer will inherit the kingdom of God [see Revelation 21:8; 1 Corinthians 6:9–10].

And one thing that will help you is if you can try to rid yourself of the thought that God is like that old man in the sky that's reaching over a cloud to touch fingers with Adam. That's horrible. He's nothing like that. Think of lightning. The scariest lightning you've ever seen on the biggest, scariest cloud, and that's just part of God's creation, and you have to face him on judgment day—and you have used his name to cuss many times. So, you should let the fear of God fill your heart because the fear of God is the beginning of wisdom. The Scriptures say, "Through the fear of the LORD, men depart from sin" [Proverbs 16:6, author's paraphrase].

It's not a matter of you saying, "Boy, it'd be a difficult decision to make." It's a matter of you thinking, *I'll have to give up pornography, and I love it. I have to give up fornication with my gorgeous girlfriend, and I love it.* But that's your choice: everlasting life or the pleasures of sin for a season. Can you hear what I'm saying?

JOHNNY: Yes.

RAY: Think of why I'm talking to you like this. I'm pleading with you as though you're on the edge of a cliff walking forward blindly, and I'm saying, "Turn around! Turn around!" This is your soul! This is your eternity! Remember the words of Jesus, "What will it a profit a man if he gains the whole world, and loses his own soul?" [Mark 8:36]. So you're going to think seriously about what we talked about?

JOHNNY: Yes.

RAY: I just did my best to hang you out of the plane by your ankles to put a little fear of God in your heart, so you'll really say, "This is such a serious business; this is my precious life, more precious than my eyes…" Do you have a Bible at home?

JOHNNY: Yes, I do.

Humility is the indicator as to whether I ask someone if I can pray for them. A truly humble person is only concerned about what God thinks. A proud person would be concerned with what people think.

RAY: Would you be embarrassed if I pray with you?

JOHNNY: No, no, of course not.

RAY: Father, I pray for Johnny. Thank you for his open heart today. I pray he will think seriously about what we talked about. I pray he will think about his secret sins—the things done in darkness—and the fear of God will fill his heart, and he'll depart from sin and fling himself upon the Savior, upon Jesus, and find everlasting life because you're rich in mercy, because you're good and kind. In Jesus' name we pray, amen.

JOHNNY: Amen.

I really liked Johnny and could feel the battle going on for his soul. He was tall, strong, and good-looking in the manliest sense. Most of us wouldn't have the temptations he no doubt had. Better to be short, weak, and not too attractive and end up in heaven than to fall like tall

Saul. The king was head and shoulders above everyone in Israel, as well as strikingly handsome (see 1 Samuel 9:2), but he ended up battling with demons. Hollywood is filled with such stories. That's why I prayed that Johnny would see the danger of his sin and run to Jesus in humility.

CHAPTER 9

THE INSTRUCTION BOOK

I have learned to ignore my initial thoughts whenever I approach someone to whom I intend to speak. This is because my thoughts often carry a mixture of natural prejudice and fear. Prejudice because (like most of us) I tend to sum up a person by their looks. God looks upon the heart, but you and I are restricted to seeing only the outward appearance, and I have found that my summations are wrong more often than not. What looks like a quiet and, more than likely, a boring person often turns out to be someone colorful and thoughtful.

My criterion is to go into all the world and preach the gospel to *every* creature even if not everyone is comfortable with or suited for being on camera.

So I ignore those prejudicial tendencies we all have. I also ignore my fears. I have a mission, and I refuse to be deterred by a selfish fear of rejection. My concerns for myself have to be dwarfed by my concern for the Goliath fate of the lost. Firefighters run into the flames because they have the equipment to fight them. Love clothes us with the ability to overcome the flames of fear.

Pablo was playing basketball by himself, and when I approached him, he immediately stopped and showed interest in what I had to say. Being on a bike with a cute white dog that is wearing red sunglasses tends to stir people's interest. His keen interest quickly dissipated my fears.

RAY: Do you think God has given an instruction book to humanity?

PABLO: The correct answer would be yes, with the Bible, but we're still screwed up. The Bible is still out there, and we're all still screwed up.

This was encouraging. It seemed that Pablo had respect for the Bible. That was a huge plus because it added instant credibility to the gospel.

RAY: That's because we're not reading the instruction book. We're trying to put the appliance together ourselves. That's why the world's in such a mess. You know the Sermon on the Mount? Jesus said one sentence that is the key to absolute harmony and happiness for all humanity, but we take no notice. Do you know what that sentence is?

PABLO: No.

RAY: He said, "Do to others as you'd have them do to you" [Matthew 7:12, author's paraphrase]. That's how to make a marriage work, that's how to make a business work, and that's how to have no road rage. If you do to other people as you'd have them do to you, you'll never lie, you'll never steal, you won't commit adultery with your neighbor's wife, you'll never kill someone. You won't even hate him…if you just do that. But we can't do it because we don't have that sort of love. We're selfish creatures. That's why marriages break down. That's why we have problems with road rage and problems with the nations. Nations won't trust each other—

PABLO: I agree.

RAY: So, I think you should read the instruction book. It tells you how to live forever. Did you know that?

PABLO: No, I did not know that, but I guess maybe I'll start reading the instructions. [Laughs]

RAY: Do you know what the cause of death is, according to the Bible?

PABLO: No.

RAY: Wages. Did you know that?

PABLO: No.

RAY: The Bible says, "The wages of sin is death" [Romans 6:23]. God's going to pay you in death for your sins. It's like a judge sees a heinous criminal; he's committed multiple murders, and the judge says, "You've *earned* the death sentence. This is your wages. This is what's due to you. This is what we're paying you." And sin is so serious to a holy God that he's given us capital punishment: "The soul who sins shall die" [Ezekiel 18:20]. "The wages of sin is death." Do you think you are so evil that God is justified in putting you to death?

PABLO: No, I don't consider myself evil.

RAY: Do you know why?

PABLO: Maybe because we don't see our own tales.

RAY: That's so good. The book of Proverbs says, "Every man is pure in his own eyes" [16:2, author paraphrase]. We always think we're right. It's human nature. "We're so pure." That's because we don't judge ourselves by God's standards. Let me share a little analogy with you. A girl was looking at a sheep as it ate green grass and thought, *How nice and white the sheep looks.* Then it began to snow, and she said, "What a dirty sheep." Same sheep, different background. When you compare yourself to man's standard, Pablo, you're a good guy. But when you compare yourself to the snowy-white righteousness of *God's* standard, you'll see yourself in truth. So, do you know what God's standard of righteousness is?

PABLO: No.

RAY: You actually do. You know what it is? The Ten Commandments. And they're written on your heart via your conscience. The word *conscience* means "with knowledge." You have an intuitive knowledge that it's wrong to murder, wrong to lie, wrong to steal, wrong to commit adultery, it's wrong to blaspheme—all those commandments are echoed by your conscience. So, we'll go through the commandments and see how you're going to do on judgment day. Can you be honest with me?

PABLO: I can be honest with you.

After reading the last several chapters, you may have noticed two things. First, I stay with a structured, biblically based presentation. I say the same thing almost every time. I'm very aware of the repetition, but I'm also aware that this is the first time the person to whom I'm speaking may have ever heard these words. I'm also cognizant of the fact that evangelistic videos and books, like the ones my ministry, Living Waters, produces, train those who watch or read them, and repetition is the mother of learning. I never expect Christians to copy what I do word for word, but I am encouraged when I hear of Christians understanding that the way to reach the lost is to go through the law.

The second thing you may have noticed is that I don't use all ten of the Ten Commandments when speaking to a lost person. This is because certain sins are more easily recognized by a sinner. Sometimes I mention the first and the second commandment when I detect the presence of idolatry. But I normally confine it to four—lying, stealing, blasphemy, and adultery of the heart. When there is self-righteousness, I bring out more ammunition and mention that God considers hatred to be murder of the heart (see 1 John 3:15), and sometimes I point out the sin of parental dishonor. I model this structure off what Jesus did. He used five of the commandments with the rich man: "You know the commandments: 'Do not commit adultery,' 'Do not murder,' 'Do not steal,' 'Do not bear false witness,' 'Do not defraud,' 'Honor your father and your mother'" (Mark 10:19).

It's interesting to note that Jesus did add, "Do not defraud." This isn't one of the Ten Commandments, but perhaps he mentioned it in case the rich young ruler gained his riches by illegal means.

James used two commandments to bring the knowledge of sin:

> If you really fulfill the royal law according to the Scripture, "You shall love your neighbor as yourself," you do well; but if you show partiality, you commit sin, and are convicted by the law as transgressors. For whoever shall keep the whole law, and yet stumble in one point, he is guilty of all. For He who said, "Do not commit adultery," also said, "Do not murder." Now if you do not commit adultery, but you do murder, you have become a transgressor of the law. So speak and so do as those who will be judged by the law of liberty. (James 2:8–12)

The Bible reveals the commandments are key to showing people their need for Jesus, the only one who can save them from the fate they deserve.

RAY: How many lies have you told in your life?
PABLO: Plenty.
RAY: What do you call someone who's told lies?
PABLO: A liar.

RAY: So, what are you?

PABLO: A liar.

RAY: Still think you're a good person?

PABLO: It makes me see that sheep in the white snow.

RAY: Yes, it's starting to snow now, isn't it?

PABLO: [Laughs]

RAY: Have you ever stolen something?

PABLO: Yes.

RAY: What do you call someone who steals things?

PABLO: A thief.

RAY: So, what are you?

PABLO: A thief.

RAY: No, you're not. You're a lying thief.

PABLO: [Laughs] Yes.

RAY: Have you ever used God's name in vain?

PABLO: Yes.

I spoke to Pablo in March 2022, just after *The Batman* movie had been released. It had no sex scenes or any nudity. There was little alcohol use and not a sniff of anyone smoking cigarettes. Movieguide added to the excitement by saying that it contained a "strong redemptive, morally uplifting worldview with biblical values." They said it "shows justice, hope, grace, faith, sacrifice, duty, goodness…with a few positive references to Christianity."[11]

Jesus is even featured in it twenty-one times. It is so subtle many hardly even noticed. *The Batman* used the name of Jesus twenty-one times *in blasphemy*.[12] The makers of the film equated Jesus with a cuss word.

When I hear someone using the name of Jesus in place of a filth word, it horrifies me. This is because I am terrified for the person using it in such a way. Jesus warned that people would have to give an account for mere idle words on judgment day. How much more will they have to give an account for the evil of blasphemy! Look at the warning: "You shall not take the name of the LORD your God in vain, *for the LORD will not hold him guiltless who takes His name in vain*" (Exodus 20:7, emphasis added).

Of course, there are always some who say that "God" is not his name. It's just his title; therefore, using it as a cuss word is not blasphemy. But if I say, "I despise the governor of this state," I'm not saying his name; I'm just using his title—the governor. His name and his title are one in the same. They are synonymous. And it's the same with the One who gave us life. His name and his title are one and the same. They are synonymous.

Blasphemy reveals how evil people hate God without cause. That hate him for the same reason criminals hate the police—because they love the darkness and hate the light. Jesus said, "The world...hates Me because I testify of it that its works are evil" (John 7:7). Blasphemy is a way for them to express their love of evil and despise that which is good.

> RAY: Would you use your mother's name as a cuss word? You hit your thumb with a hammer; you want to say [a swear word]. Would you use your mother's name in the place of that word?
>
> PABLO: No, I wouldn't. Well now, you're putting it in a whole different aspect.

Each of us intuitively knows it's wrong to take God's name in vain because of the presence of our God-given conscience.

Never underestimate the influence of that inner knowledge as you take sinners through the law. Again, it will side with you if you speak to them of each commandment, affirming its truth. Look at this portion of Scripture, which tells us how God has written his law on our hearts (via the conscience) and what it does within the human mind:

> When Gentiles, who do not have the Law [since it was given only to Jews], do instinctively the things the Law requires [guided only by their conscience], they are a law to themselves,

though they do not have the Law. They show that the essential requirements of the Law are written in their hearts; and their conscience [their sense of right and wrong, their moral choices] bearing witness and their thoughts alternately accusing or perhaps defending them on that day when, as my gospel proclaims, God will judge the secrets [all the hidden thoughts and concealed sins] of men through Christ Jesus. (Romans 2:14–16 AMP)

The voice of a guilty conscience can be like sudden thunder. It can have the effect of immediately sobering us, awakening us to the seriousness nature of blasphemy.

RAY: You'd never do that with your mother's name, but you've done it with *God's* name, who gave you your mother. "Hallowed be thy name" [Matthew 6:9 KJV]. God's name is holy, and you have substituted it for [a swear] word to express disgust. It's called blasphemy. Very serious. I appreciate your honesty. Jesus said, "If you look at a woman and lust for her, you commit adultery with her in your heart" [Matthew 5:28, author paraphrase]. Have you ever looked at a woman with lust?

PABLO: Yes.

RAY: Have you had sex before marriage?

PABLO: Yes.

RAY: So this is for you to judge yourself, as the snow comes down. Pablo, you've told me you're a lying, thieving, fornicating, blasphemous adulterer at heart, and you have to face God on judgment day. If he judges you by those commandments, are you going to be innocent or guilty?

PABLO: Guilty as charged.

RAY: You've *earned* your wages. Heaven or hell?

PABLO: Going by what we were just talking about, probably hell.

RAY: Does that concern you?

PABLO: I guess not because I kept doing it, right?

RAY: Up until now. Now you've been confronted with the law. Your conscience has done its duty. So, something in you should be saying "Whoa! What should I do to be saved?"

PABLO: Yes, of course, it's going through my mind.

Did you ever hear such wonderful words? Pablo was asking (in his mind) how he can be saved. When I go through the often-uncomfortable task of revealing someone's sin using the law, this is the desired effect. After King David committed adultery and murder, God used Nathan to expose his sin (see 2 Samuel 12). In the book of Psalms, we are privy to his intimate prayer of repentance. Notice how he *owned* his sin, that there wasn't a hint of self-justification. There was no trivializing of his crimes. Notice also that he was throwing himself on the mercy of the judge, trusting in his "tender" mercies. And then note his concession:

> Have mercy upon me, O God,
> According to Your lovingkindness;
> According to the multitude of Your tender mercies,
> Blot out my transgressions.
> Wash me thoroughly from my iniquity,
> And cleanse me from my sin.
> For I acknowledge my transgressions,
> And my sin is always before me.
> Against You, You only, have I sinned,
> And done this evil in Your sight—
> That You may be found just when You speak,
> And blameless when You judge. (Psalm 51:1–4)

David conceded that he was in the wrong and that God was right. The judge was just and blameless. That's the conclusion to which a sinner must come before he or she will embrace the gospel. Why put on a parachute if I'm still convinced that I'm in no danger? That God is totally justified in damning us in hell is a huge turnaround from "I'm a good person…everybody sins…it was in the past."

Again, this is a huge change of mind, but this shift can happen regularly in the lives of unrepentant people if we faithfully use the law to reveal sin and trust in the Holy Spirit to convict them of sin. This is what Jesus said about the Holy Spirit convicting us of our sins: "Nevertheless I tell you the truth; it is expedient for you that I go away: for if I go not away, the Comforter will not come unto you; but if I depart, I will send him unto you. And when he is come, he will reprove the world of sin, and of righteousness, and of judgment" (John 16:7–8 KJV). We're never alone in battle, and we are fully equipped to overcome the enemy.

> RAY: There's a jailer in the book of Acts in the Bible who was in an earthquake, and he turned to the disciples and said, "What must I do to be saved?" [Acts 16:30]. It wasn't the earthquake that freaked him out. It was the fact that the earthquake opened up the jail doors for the disciples to leave. That freaked him out because he was aware that there's a God who cares [about sin]. So do you know what God did for guilty sinners so we wouldn't have to go to hell?

He did something so we can be saved from the earthquake of his wrath. You know what he did?

PABLO: He sacrificed himself.

RAY: Yes, most people know that, but they don't know this: the Ten Commandments are called the moral law. You and I broke the law. Jesus paid the fine. That's why he said, "It is finished," just before he died [John 19:30]. Pablo, that's a weird thing to say just as you're dying—"It is finished." But he was saying that the debt has been paid.

It's like a judge in a court of law can let you go even though you're guilty and have speeding fines. He can say, "Pablo, there's a stack of speeding fines here; this is deadly serious. Someone's paid them. You're out of here." And he can do that which is legal. Someone paid your fine; you can leave the courtroom. And, because Jesus paid our fine in full, we can leave the courtroom on judgment day. God can take the death sentence off us, as he took our sin upon himself. "God commended[eth] his love toward us, in that, while we were yet sinners, Christ died for us" [Romans 5:8 KJV], and then he rose from the dead. The Bible says, "It was not possible that death could hold him" [Acts 2:24, author's paraphrase].

And Pablo, you just have to simply obey the command to repent and trust in Jesus... Just go straight to God and say, "Dear God, I've sinned against you. I've been drinking iniquity like water. My heart is wicked. I deserve judgment, but you're rich in mercy, and I plead with you: please grant me your mercy." And the Bible says, "He's rich in mercy to all that call upon him" [Psalm 86:5, author's paraphrase]. And then trust in Jesus like you a trust in a parachute.

At the moment, you're trusting in your goodness to save you. Transfer your trust from yourself to the Savior. It's like if you're going to jump out of a plane, you wouldn't trust yourself to save yourself by flapping your arms. It's a ten-thousand-foot drop. You trust the parachute. If you'll do that, you've got God's promise (and he cannot lie because he's without sin—it's impossible for God to lie). He'll forgive every secret sin, every sin done in darkness and in the light. He'll forgive them in a second. Not because of your goodness but because he's rich in mercy, and he's filled with amazing grace. Is this making sense?

PABLO: It's making sense.

RAY: You going to think about what we talked about today?

PABLO: Oh yes. Sure I am.

RAY: Do you have a Bible at home?

PABLO: I sure do.

RAY: Would you mind if I pray with you?

PABLO: No, I don't mind.

RAY: Father, I pray for Pablo…thank you for a divine encounter today, that you brought us together, and I thank you for his open and honest heart. May this day he truly repent and trust in Jesus and pass from death to life because of your mercy. In Jesus' name we pray, amen. Can I give you a little Gospel of John?

PABLO: Sure.

RAY: Okay, let me grab it for you. [Hands Pablo the Gospel of John] Pablo, great to talk to you today. I really appreciate it, and I'm so pleased you're going to think about this.

PABLO: It was a pleasure.

How blessed we are to have the Bible. It's not only God's love letter to humanity, but it really is also a lamp to our feet and a light to our path. Because of God's Word, we know where we are going. But even more than that, from Genesis to Revelation, Scripture answers the *Why Jesus?* question. Look at what Luke says about the Scriptures and Jesus: "And beginning at Moses and all the Prophets, He expounded to them in all the Scriptures the things concerning Himself" (24:27). From the beginning to the end, God has been revealing his plan to bring humanity into a relationship with him—a plan centered on Jesus.

CHAPTER 10

THE WORLD'S VOICE

I once asked myself, *What were the moral and social issues that plagued contemporary society during the book of Acts?* The answer was that I didn't know, and the reason I didn't know was because the book of Acts doesn't specifically mention the church confronting the issues of abortion, spousal abuse, human trafficking, sexual sins, slavery, rape, or pedophilia. Some of these are spoken of in other parts of Scripture, so we know they existed.

This is a gentle reminder of our agenda. Christians haven't been winning the battle against many of the major moral issues of the day—such as abortion and sexual sins. It seems that the world's voice is bigger and louder than ours. For example, YouTube says,

> YouTube is an open video platform where
> anyone can upload a video and share it with
> the world. With this openness comes incredible

opportunities, as well as challenges—which is why we're always working to balance creative expression with our responsibility to protect the community from harmful content. At the heart of our approach are the four Rs: we Remove content that violates our policies as quickly as possible, Reduce the spread of harmful misinformation and content that brushes up against our policy lines, Raise up authoritative sources when people are looking for news and information, and Reward trusted, eligible Creators and artists.[13]

"Harmful content" to the world can mean issues that are morally offensive to God, but there's a silver lining with this censorship. It's causing us to fall back on our greatest offensive weapon: the gospel.

These social issues are just the bad fruit that issue from sin. And only the gospel can kill its root. If we forget that, we aren't fighting the good fight of faith. Instead, we are in another battle—one that is fought on another hill—the hill of morality. We must instead make a stand on the hill of Calvary. That's the battle we can't lose because our weapons are not carnal but mighty through God's pulling down of strongholds. The gospel is the weapon that puts the beginning of the end to sin. It has done that with every Christian, and it can do it with this evil world.

So if someone says that he's sexually confused, it's not necessary to tell him that sexual sin disgusts the Lord. That's going to poke him in the eye when you want to feed him in the mouth. Just set aside that thought and instead take him through the moral law. This is because 1 Timothy 1:8–10 tells us that God's law was made for him and all those whose actions are "contrary to sound doctrine" (v. 10). You want him to see that all sin disgusts the Lord. You will achieve the same goal but from a different direction. Again, you don't need to climb the hill of morality. Instead, head for Calvary's hill. That's because you don't want to win an argument. You, rather, want to win him to Christ because you love him and want to see him in heaven.

One aspect of evangelism that people find both terrifying and heartbreaking is the reality that not everyone you speak to will be receptive to knowing the truth about their sin and what Jesus did for them. Sometimes people find the world's voice more persuasive than Calvary's hill. This chapter contains three conversations with people who weren't open to hearing the gospel. They were so comfortable in their own beliefs about God and the world that they—at the time I spoke to them—seemed unwilling to hear the truth.

As you will see, this father and his son were confident atheists.

RAY: Do you think there is an afterlife?

FATHER: I have no idea.

RAY: Do you ever think about it?

FATHER: Once in a while.

RAY [TO SON]: And what about you?

SON: That's a very difficult question. But it's also loaded, so, I think, no.

RAY: Do you ever think about it?

SON: I've been thinking about it since I was seven.

RAY: Well, [George Harrison] said the most important thing in life is to seek God. Do you agree with that?

FATHER: I'm an atheist, so you'd probably not get that from me. [Laughs]

RAY [TO SON]: What about you…are you an atheist?

SON: I am as well, yes.

RAY: Interesting shirt, what does it say? [His T-shirt has a picture of Satan on it.]

SON: *El diablito.* My girlfriend got it for me.

RAY [TO FATHER]: Do you really believe the scientific impossibility that nothing created everything?

This question is extremely effective with atheists. The Bible says that they are fools, but the Scriptures add that they think that they are intelligent.

The fool has said in his heart,
"There is no God."
They are corrupt,
they have done abominable works,
there is none who does good.
(Psalm 14:1)

For the wrath of God is revealed from heaven against all ungodliness and unrighteousness of men, who suppress the truth in unrighteousness, because what may be known of God is manifest in them, for God has shown it to them. For since the creation of the world His invisible attributes are clearly seen, being understood by the things that are made, even His eternal power and Godhead, so that they are without excuse, because, although they knew God, they did not glorify Him as God, nor were thankful, but became futile in their thoughts, and their foolish hearts were darkened. *Professing to be wise, they became fools*. (Romans 1:18–22, emphasis added)

Look at how these verses give us insight into the mind and the hidden motive of professing atheists:

1. They suppress the truth in unrighteousness.
2. They intuitively know God exists because of conscience and because of creation and are, therefore, without excuse.
3. Even though they have this knowledge, they refuse to glorify God or be thankful for his many blessings. The result of this is a darkened heart.
4. Even though they are fools, they profess to be wise.

How evident is this last statement! Atheists *really* do think that they are society's intellectual elite. They are a cut above the billions of unthinking theists. But watch the father backpedal after being confronted with the foolishness of atheism:

> FATHER: If you characterize it like that, I don't know. I just don't have enough to believe in one higher power creating all of this. It's highly unlikely, to me. That's just my own personal belief. It's just easiest.

So now he wasn't an atheist. He had defaulted to not knowing if God exists, which is a huge leap from believing without a doubt there is no God. Then he insinuated that this higher power doesn't have enough power to create all things, saying that it's highly unlikely

THE WORLD'S VOICE • 173

that God does. And finally he conceded that just didn't
want to consider God existing.

RAY: Atheism is easiest?

FATHER: Like Jesus was here to save us all, and
you see people getting exploited, murdered.
God is all powerful, yet everybody's out here
getting exploited, taken advantage of. I'm just
kind of cool on one religion telling me they
got the answer for everything. Not saying that
I have the answer, but I'm sure as hell don't
believe *they* have it. No pun intended.

RAY: Could you repeat that?

FATHER: *I'm sure as hell* don't believe they…

RAY: Do you really believe…

FATHER: [Sighs]

RAY: That was a big sigh, wasn't it?

FATHER: Yes, I just feel like this is a…

RAY: Am I annoying you?

FATHER: This is a…you're trying to convert.

SON: Organized religion has always caused
mass war and mass atrocities.

RAY: It's six percent of wars. Did you
know that? It's six percent according to the
Encyclopedia of Wars.

According to the *Encyclopedia of Wars*, out of all 1,763 known and recorded historical conflicts, 121, or 6.87 percent, had religion as their primary cause.[14]

FATHER AND SON: [Start walking away]

RAY: Can I give you guys a gift?

SON: [Still walking away] Americans have now been in wars over 70 percent of their lifetime as a country. Take that into consideration as a Christian.

It's no fun having someone walk away when you're still talking to them. Our consolation is that the rich young ruler walked away from Jesus (see Mark 10:22), and if that happened to Jesus, we shouldn't be surprised when it happens to us. If you're bucked off a horse, the best thing you can do for yourself is to quickly get back on another horse.

Dolores was a very sweet, elderly woman. Like the father and son, she was unwilling to hear any beliefs that conflicted with her own.

RAY: Do you think there is an afterlife?

DOLORES: The afterlife? Now that I'm in my eighties, I believe that we just die. I saw an interview with Larry King, and I can't remember…the guy that created all the puppets.

RAY: Jim Henson.

DOLORES: Yes, Jim Henson. He agreed; he said that they both believe that there's no heaven, that they don't really know what happens.

RAY: You know, Jim Henson died young. It was a shock to everybody, and I'm sure to himself. But now he knows there's an afterlife and same with Larry King. Larry King was tormented by the fear of death. He kept talking about it all the time as he got older. You don't want to leave yourself without hope. Do you ever read the Bible?

DOLORES: No, I don't.

RAY: The Bible is God's instruction book. It tells you how to find everlasting life. What do you think it says?

DOLORES: I have no idea.

RAY: Well, shouldn't you find out? Shouldn't you look into it? It's the world's biggest-selling book of all time.

DOLORES: Yes, well, that's your belief.

Often when people say, "Well, that's your belief," it's another way of saying, "I'm not interested in what you have to say." The door is being closed in your face, and there's nothing much you can do about it other than to respect their wishes. When it happens to me, I try to show respect and kindness. When Dolores

walked away from me just after this statement, I offered
her a gift card, and she turned around and came back.
I was then able to give her one of my books, which she
assured me that she would read. That was heartening to
me in what would normally have been a discouraging
conversation.

> RAY: Well, that's a fact, it's the world's biggest-
> selling book of all time, and it's the most hated
> book in the world and the most loved. You
> know why it's hated?
>
> DOLORES: Uh, I got to go, bye. [Turns around
> to leave]
>
> RAY: Well, nice to talk to you, Dolores. Can I
> give you a couple of In-N-Out [Burger] cards?
>
> DOLORES: Sure. [Turns back around]
>
> RAY: [Laughs] Okay. That turned you back,
> didn't it? If In-N-Out can get you to turn
> around, God's promise of everlasting life should
> do the same for you, okay?

Matt was middle-aged and very confident in his
remarks. Most people admit that they have no idea
what happens after death. Not Matt. He was adamant
that death is the end. But what seemed like a closed
door needn't be.

> RAY: Do you think there is an afterlife?

MATT: No, I don't. We're a cosmic accident, and when we're done, we're done.

RAY: So what caused the accident?

MATT: The life thing, if you look at the odds, it's like a one in a million, but it only had to happen once, and then it just builds from there. At one point the universe was tiny, tiny, tiny.

RAY: And where did that come from?

MATT: And then it blew up.

RAY: Where did the "tiny, tiny, tiny" come from?

MATT: The same way it's going to go tiny again.

RAY: But where did it come from? What was the initial cause?

MATT: Oh, it doesn't matter.

RAY: Of course it does. It does to me. I'm a thinking person.

MATT: Anything that happened prior to the big bang has no effect on anything after the big bang. So there's no purpose in worrying about it.

RAY: So the big bang is still credible? I've heard that it's been discredited.

MATT: Because it's not a "bang." Everything was tiny, tiny, and then now it's expanding. When it hits a certain expansion, I believe it's going to start shrinking back down again.

RAY: That sounds like Disney to me, like a little fairy [puff noise] and everything happened. Is that what you think?

MATT: Sure.

I couldn't help but be cynical because of his insistence that the entire universe started out as something that was "tiny, tiny" with no first cause. My mocking his statement wasn't done in anger but with a smile. Jesus told the religious leaders that they strained a gnat and swallowed a camel. This was a gnat and camel moment. Also, I could feel that Matt didn't mind a sword fight. My sense about this was confirmed by his following remarks.

RAY: Are you an atheist?

MATT: Yes.

RAY: So, you believe the scientific impossibility that nothing created everything? That's utterly impossible.

See now as Matt was confronted with the infeasibility of atheism and reconsidered it.

MATT: No, I believe there was something at the beginning. You want to make up a fairy-tale that there's some afterlife or some big cosmic person watching over you. If that makes you feel better, good for you. But there's no proof; there's no reason to believe it and…nah.

He now revealed he may not be an atheist by saying "there was something at the beginning" and hinted that his disbelief was really about God's moral requirements by referring to God as "some big cosmic person watching over you" as if he were a parent always ready to discipline. The reason why many who claim to oppose God's existence actually oppose their need to follow the moral law is explained in Romans 8:7: "The mind of the flesh [with its sinful pursuits] is actively hostile to God. It does not submit itself to God's law, since it cannot" (AMP). Those who rebel against God cannot submit themselves to his law.

> RAY: Could it be, Matt, that you don't like the thought of God because he speaks of morality and moral responsibility and says certain things are right and certain things are wrong. Could it be that? Could it be that you like your pornography and fornication, and any thought of God makes you think, *Man, I'm responsible to him.* Would that be right?
>
> MATT: No, I believe that if you need God to be a moral person, you're not a moral person to begin with. I'm a moral person. I act in moral ways, and I don't need some cosmic parent

who's going to spank me if I do something bad. If the only reason you're not out raping and murdering is because God told you not to, you're a [expletive] person.

At this point, I didn't tell Matt why a Christian refrains from sin. He thought it's because we are afraid that God will punish us, not understanding that our punishment has already fallen on the Savior. But this explanation wouldn't make sense to him at this point because he didn't see how his sin separates him from Jesus. Rather, he was opening a door for me by saying, "I act in moral ways." That was an invitation I gladly accepted.

RAY: So, you're a moral person?

MATT: Yes.

RAY: By what standard?

MATT: The human standard. It evolves over time. We live in a community.

RAY: Okay, so I'm going to give you a standard to judge yourself by. Can you be honest?

MATT: Let's go. Is this like...how much longer we got here?

RAY: I'll be really quick.

MATT: Okay.

Each of us should practice what we preach. You never know how much time you will have with someone. Practice a Zacchaeus presentation for those who are waiting for a bus and a Methuselah presentation for those who are sitting next to you on a long flight on a plane. Always be ready.

RAY: How many lies have you told in your life? This is the Ten Commandments we're looking at.

MATT: I don't know.

RAY: Quite a few?

MATT: For a while there, yes. I made a point several years ago of not lying anymore. So, I quit lying years ago.

RAY: Have you ever stolen something?

MATT: Nope.

RAY: Is that one of those lies?

MATT: I don't remember having ever stolen something. How's that?

RAY: You've forgotten what you stole?

MATT: Because I don't steal, so I probably didn't.

RAY: You *probably* didn't? You weren't watching closely?

We may think that we've forgotten certain things that happened, especially when it seems like it happened one hundred years ago, but a song on the radio can suddenly bring them back. These memories can often be pleasant. But when we sin, we unwittingly put a marker on that event—because the conscience was involved. These memories aren't so pleasant, so we tend to silence them.

> MATT: You remember every second of your life?
>
> RAY: Sure, I do. I remember when I stole. It stays in the conscience.
>
> MATT: Oh well, then I didn't steal because it's not in my conscience. So clearly, I didn't steal.
>
> RAY: Okay, third question. Have you ever used God's name in vain?
>
> MATT: Sure.
>
> RAY: Would you use your mother's name as a cuss word?
>
> MATT: Yes, she's not a nice person.

This shouldn't have shocked me, but it did. However, my consolation was that, by admitting that he would do such a horrible thing, he had just stepped in front of another loaded cannon. It was more ammunition to show Matt that he had sinned against God. People are more likely to surrender if they are looking down the barrel of five loaded cannons.

RAY: You've just broken the fifth commandment: "Honor your father and mother."

MATT: Yes, but if your father [expletive], they don't get to be honored just because [expletive].

This clearly stirred a little passion. But what Matt didn't realize is that our obedience to the fifth commandment doesn't depend upon our parents being *worthy* of our honor. None of us is worthy. We honor our parents because God commands us to honor them.

RAY: Jesus said, "If you look at a woman and lust for her, you commit adultery with her in your heart" [Matthew 5:28, author paraphrase]. Have you ever looked at a woman with lust?

MATT: Oh yes. All the time.

RAY: Have you had sex before marriage?

MATT: Loads of times and after marriage.

Again, even though this was a verbal sword fight with Matt, I spoke with love and a gentle but firm tone. There was no anger or impatience. If he detected either, he may have become defensive and become angry himself. Fire begets fire. So, here comes evidence that I care about him, with my appreciation of his honesty and the deliberate use of Matt's name.

RAY: Okay, that's adultery. So, here's a quick summation. I appreciate your honesty, Matt.

MATT: Sure.

RAY: You've just told me you're a lying, thieving (because I can't believe you've never stolen something), fornicating, blasphemous adulterer at heart, and you've got to face God on judgment day, whether you believe in him or not. If he judges you by the Ten Commandments, and I've said, "If."

If can be a very effective door opener that keeps the conversation going. Without it, Matt would almost certainly have said, "I don't believe in judgment day." That can be a slammed door. *If* puts the foot in and keeps it open.

RAY: Do you think you'll be innocent or guilty?

MATT: No, if he judges me by that [expletive] set of rules, I'm definitely guilty.

RAY: Heaven or hell?

MATT: I mean obviously if I'm guilty, and it's all real, and I'm wrong, then hell. Like, if I'm wrong, I know where I'm going, and that's fine because I'm not wrong.

RAY: It doesn't concern you?

MATT: Not at all.

RAY: Matt, it horrifies me, the thought of death seizing upon you and you being justly damned in hell. That horrifies me. You don't realize this, but I love you. I care about you, and the thought of you going to hell takes my breath away. What did God do for guilty sinners so we wouldn't have to go to hell?

MATT: Yes, I know, he sacrificed his kid. That's like taking all the debt in the world, putting it on one guy, and then killing him, and now no one else has any debt. It's a [expletive] way to do things.

RAY: If I had your theology, I'd be an atheist. That is so erroneous. God became a human being, suffered, and died for the sins of the world. We broke God's law. Jesus paid the fine. That means God can dismiss your case. He can forgive your sins and let you live forever...

MATT: Or if he was almighty and all powerful, he could just make it all rainbows and [expletive] butterflies. If he could do it, why isn't he? Why did he have to sacrifice himself and cause pain and suffering to himself to save us from some [expletive]? He's almighty and all powerful and he could just do it, like he's stronger than Thanos. [Thanos is a supervillain appearing in American comic books published by Marvel Comics.] He could "Snap!"

RAY: Because he's just and holy, and he's going make sure justice is done.

MATT: [Sniggers] Okay.

RAY: I want you to repent and trust Christ so you can have everlasting life. I want you to think about what we talked about. Will you at least think about it when you leave?

MATT: The same way I'll think about Santa Claus and the Easter bunny. They're fun little stories.

RAY: Hey, thanks for talking to me. I appreciate it.

MATT: Yes, have a nice day. It was fun.

RAY: I want to give you something.

MATT: Okay. Is it a Bible? Because I don't want a Bible.

RAY: No, no, no, it's a couple of In-N-Out cards for lunch.

MATT: Oh, thank you!

While it's a joy to speak to someone who is open to the gospel, we should never hesitate to speak to someone who is prepared to listen, even though they don't seem to be open. We don't know what's going on in somebody's heart of hearts. Those who put up the biggest fight are often those who are feeling convicted by the Holy Spirit for their sins. That's why they're fighting. So never be discouraged and never hesitate to be steadfast in sharing the good news with anyone who will listen.

If reading this book has caused you to question your salvation, please don't hesitate to put the book down and ask God to forgive your sins. Thoroughly confess them to the Lord. Make Psalm 51 your personal prayer. And then trust alone in Jesus for your eternal salvation. There's nothing more tragic than dying in your sins and being "almost" saved. That would be like jumping out of a plane at ten thousand feet and almost putting on a parachute. So repent and trust in Jesus today. Make your calling and election sure; as the Bible says, "Brethren, be even more diligent to make your call and election sure, for if you do these things you will never stumble; for so an entrance will be supplied to you abundantly into the everlasting kingdom of our Lord and Savior Jesus Christ" (2 Peter 1:10–11).

CHAPTER 11

FORGIVENESS ISN'T AUTOMATIC

In the following interview, Terri talked about God not condemning *anyone*, not even Hitler. This woman's belief about the nature of God was not only unbiblical, but it was also completely illogical. And yet it's very common. As you encounter people like Terri, think of A. W. Tozer's powerful quote: "The vague and tenuous hope that God is too kind to punish the ungodly has become a deadly opiate for the consciences of millions."[15]

> RAY: Do you think there's an afterlife?
>
> TERRI: I do. I think there's a heaven. I believe there is a heaven.
>
> RAY: Do you believe in God?
>
> TERRI: I believe in God, yes.
>
> RAY: Do you believe in a hell?

TERRI: I believe there are people who don't go to heaven, and I'm not sure about hell. I'm not sure that you go down with the demons and with the devil. I don't know that I believe that.

Our concept of what God will do with evil men and women is determined by our concept of his character. The psalmist puts his finger on the two-fold problem:

> But to the wicked God says:
> "What right have you to declare My statutes,
> or take My covenant in your mouth,
> seeing you hate instruction
> and cast My words behind you?"
> (Psalm 50:16–17)

The first problem is that sinners reject God's revelation about himself in his Word. They hate what Scripture says and cast its inspired words behind them. The fruit of this is lawlessness. They don't condemn sin. The thief and the adulterer don't believe they're sinning in the slightest:

> When you saw a thief, you consented with him,
> and have been a partaker with adulterers.
> You give your mouth to evil,
> and your tongue frames deceit.
> You sit and speak against your brother;

you slander your own mother's son.
These things you have done,
and I kept silent. (vv. 18–21)

Which brings us to the second part of the problem. They then pull God down to their own evil standard
of morality. They surmise that he is just like them.

You thought that I was altogether like you;
but I will rebuke you,
and set them in order before your eyes.
(v. 21)

Those who embrace the sin of idolatry are in for
a rude awakening.

Now consider this, you who forget God,
lest I tear you in pieces,
and there be none to deliver:
whoever offers praise glorifies Me;
and to him who orders his conduct aright
I will show the salvation of God.
(vv. 22–23)

When you distort God's character, it becomes
easy to deny the existence of God's coming judgment.
Who likes punishment? But the Bible is clear: hell is
real whether we believe it or not.

RAY: Well, do you think there's a place of punishment? Does God have a place of punishment?

TERRI: I think their punishment is not being with him, so yes.

RAY: I think they'd be thrilled not to be with him. They live a whole life raping, murdering, and hating God, and using his name as a cuss word. They'll be thrilled to end up in hell. Hell would be heaven to them if there's no God there. So, what do you think God should do with someone like Hitler?

TERRI: Forgive him and love him.

RAY: You don't think [God] cares about six million Jews that were slaughtered because of [Hitler's] policies and because of [Hitler's] beliefs?

TERRI: I do. I think he does, but I think there's a place for forgiveness for everybody.

RAY: So, everybody just gets forgiven?

TERRI: Yes.

RAY: Six million Jews [puff noise], forget it.

Those who think that God won't judge evil often don't think of the implications of their belief. What judge would let a vicious rapist walk out of court? If he's a good judge, he must see that justice is done. If he allows the rapist to go free, he's an evil judge. He's complicit with the rape and should be prosecuted himself. But watch Terri attribute a lesser sense of justice to God than to that of an evil judge. Sinners tend to hold on to their idols for dear life.

> TERRI: No, it's horrible, I know! It's horrible, I know.
>
> RAY: This is terrible.
>
> TERRI: Terrible, I agree.
>
> RAY: Any judge doesn't just forgive.
>
> TERRI: No, they don't.
>
> RAY: If a man has raped a woman and slit her throat, the judge doesn't say, "*Poof*, I forgive." He makes sure the guy goes to the electric chair or to prison for life.
>
> TERRI: Yes, but God isn't the judge, you know.
>
> RAY: Well, the Bible says he's a judge. He's the habitation of justice; we base our laws off the laws of God, the Ten Commandments…Any judge who lets a criminal go wouldn't be a good judge. We expect our judges to carry out justice. Shouldn't God be the same?
>
> TERRI: No, I agree with you with the judges and putting criminals away. God is different;

we're talking about a higher power and somebody who promises to forgive, you know? You
ask for forgiveness. He forgives you.

RAY: That's all you have to say, "God forgive me"?

TERRI: Yes, I think you do, yes.

This was a dead end. Her mind was made up—
despite her admittance that her belief that God just
forgives everyone automatically is both horrible and
terrible. She needed to see her own sin. The cannons
of God's law needed to be brought out and the fuses lit.

RAY: Have you ever heard the gospel?

TERRI: Well, like, how?

RAY: I'm going to share it with you, but before
I do, I want to tell you about a guy I saw over-
take me coming here on the freeway today, and
he really annoyed me. He was doing at least
one hundred miles an hour, and I felt angry.
But then I thought, imagine if his wife has
just called him on a cell phone and she says,
"Somebody's breaking into our home. I think
he's going to kill me!"

So, now my attitude changes because I've
gotten extra information. Now I'm sympathetic
with the guy, and I'm saying, "Put your foot
down—go for it," because the extra information

has changed everything. What I want to talk to you about is what's called the offense of the gospel. The gospel offends when you share it with people—all they need is extra information… it'll change everything. So, can you be honest with me?

TERRI: Of course.

RAY: I'm going to share the gospel with you, and let's see if it offends you. Do you think you're a good person?

TERRI: Yes.

RAY: How many lies have you told in your life?

TERRI: A gazillion.

RAY: What do you call someone who's told a gazillion lies?

TERRI: A human.

RAY: A liar.

TERRI: Okay.

RAY: So, what are you?

TERRI: A liar.

RAY: Do you still think you're a good person?

TERRI: Oh yes.

RAY: Have you ever stolen something?

TERRI: Yes.

RAY: What do you call someone who steals?

TERRI: A stealer.

RAY: A thief.

TERRI: Okay, whatever.

RAY: So, what are you?

TERRI: I'm a thief.

RAY: No, you're a lying thief.

TERRI: Okay! [Laughs]

RAY: Do you still think you're a good person?

TERRI: Yes.

RAY: Have you ever used God's name in vain?

TERRI: Yep.

RAY: Would you use your mother's name as a cuss word? You've hit your thumb with a hammer, and you want to say something disgusting like—

TERRI: It's my favorite word.

RAY: Like [a cuss] word.

TERRI: Yes.

RAY: But you use God's name in its place. Would you do that with your mother's name?

TERRI: Well, yes, I do it all the time. [Expletive] is my favorite cuss word.

RAY: Wow.

I was having trouble reconciling her disgusting, decadent language with what I saw. Terri was an attractive, well-dressed, middle-aged woman, not a thoughtless, rebellious-looking teenager.

> TERRI: I know, well, whatever. [Laughs] There's a relief to the whole word.
>
> RAY: Yes, but why would you use God's name in place of [a cuss word]?
>
> TERRI: Oh, I don't. [Expletive] is what I use.
>
> RAY: No, but have you ever used God's name in vain?
>
> TERRI: Well, sure.
>
> RAY: Okay, that's using it as a cuss word. It's using it in vain.
>
> TERRI: Yeah, it's out of habit. I know what you're saying.

Finally! I found the voice of her very dulled conscience. My hope was that her conscience was going to come out of the grave and do its God-given duty.

> RAY: It's *really* bad, Terri. Punishable by death in the Old Testament, it's so serious.
>
> TERRI: Well, I'm not going to get punished by death.

RAY: We're going personal. Jesus said that if you look with lust, you commit adultery in your heart [see Matthew 5:28]. Have you ever looked at someone with lust?

TERRI: Well, yeah, we all have.

RAY: Sex before marriage?

TERRI: Of course.

RAY: Okay, Terri, now here's the offensive part. I'm not judging you, but you've told me you're a lying, thieving, blasphemous, fornicating, mother-dishonoring adulterer at heart, and you have to face God on judgment day. And there's one more commandment that you broke. Do you know what it is?

TERRI: Nope.

RAY: The first of the Ten Commandments. Are you familiar with that one?

TERRI: Which is?

RAY: "You shall have no other gods before me," and the second goes with it: "Don't make yourself a graven image"—don't make up a false god with your hands or your mind. I did it before I was a Christian. I shaped a god to suit my sins; a cuddly, snuggly god, a nonexistent god that was a figment of my imagination because I felt comfortable with him. Because my god didn't punish sin. You'd just ask him for forgiveness, and he doesn't care about right or wrong. It's called idolatry, and the Bible says that idolaters will not inherit the kingdom of God [see 1 Corinthians 6:9–10].

So, here's the big question; this is where we're going with this before we get to the good news of the gospel. I appreciate you staying with me because what I'm saying is awkward for you and for me. Here's where I'm going… if God judges you by the Ten Commandments on judgment day—and we've looked at five of them—are you going to be innocent or guilty?

TERRI: Guilty.

RAY: Heaven or hell?

TERRI: See, I don't know that there's a hell, but I'm going to heaven because I'll always ask for forgiveness.

RAY: It's like saying to a judge, "Please forgive me." He's not going to forgive you; he's going to say, "You're going to jail," if you've committed serious crimes. Let me tell you what the Bible says. The Bible says that all liars will have their part in the lake of fire—no thief, no blasphemer, no adulterer will inherit the kingdom of God [see Revelation 21:8; 1 Corinthians 6:9–10]. Do you know what death is according to the Bible?

TERRI: What?

RAY: Wages.

TERRI: Wages?

RAY: Yes, it's wages. The Bible says, "The wages of sin is death" [Romans 6:23]. In other words, sin is so serious to God that he is paying you in death for your sins. Like a judge in a court of law looks at a heinous criminal who's raped three girls and murdered them and says, "You've *earned* the death sentence. This is your wages. This is what's due to you. This is what we're paying you." Sin is so serious to a holy God; he's given us the death sentence, capital punishment. Proof of our sin will be our death. "The soul who sins shall die" [Ezekiel 18:20]. Now, let's see how your knowledge is; what did God do for guilty sinners so we wouldn't have to go to hell?

TERRI: I don't know. What did he do?

That question was a good sign. It was a side-of-the-road billboard that said, "Your destination is straight ahead." It told me to head for the cross. She could have said that I had offended her and derailed me, but she didn't.

It is understandable that the world embraces a god that has no sense of justice, righteousness, or truth. When they deny the inspiration of Scripture, they are left to their own imaginations as to who God is like, and those imaginations can be shaped by what seems like inaction from God when it comes to injustice. Masses of people have been murdered, and there seems to be no action from heaven. Women are viciously raped, and there seems to be no action from heaven. This world explodes with evil every day, and God seems silent.

But we know from Scripture that every time somebody sins, they store up God's wrath. And that terrible wrath is going to be revealed on the day of judgment (see Romans 2:2–11). However, for those who know the gospel, we see the ultimate act of justice in the cross. How angry is God at sin? Look to the battered and bruised body of the Son of God. See his precious blood streaming from his wounds. Hear his cry of anguish: "My God, my God, why have You forsaken Me?" (Matthew 27:46) as the fury of a holy Creator comes down upon the sacrificial Lamb for our salvation. Yes, God is angry with our sins, but he has also provided payment for them.

> RAY: You actually know, but you don't understand it. Christ died on the cross for the sin of

the world. Now, we all know that, but we don't know this, and this is the game changer: the Ten Commandments are called the moral law. You and I broke the law, the Ten Commandments. Jesus paid the fine. That's what happened on that cross. That's why he said, "It is finished," just before he died [John 19:30]. In other words, the debt has been paid.

You know, if you're in court and you've broken the law and you've gotten a lot of speeding fines, the judge can let you go if someone else pays your fine. He can say, "This is a serious lot of speeding fines here, Terri, but someone's paid them. You're out of here," and he can do that which is legal and right and just. God can *legally* dismiss your case because Jesus paid the fine in his life's blood. Your sins can be forgiven. God can take the death sentence off you—not because you're good but because he's good; he's rich in mercy. It's called amazing grace…ever heard the song "Amazing Grace"?

TERRI: [Nods head yes]

RAY: Do you remember the words?

TERRI: Yes, but I'm not singing them to you.

RAY: You can say them to me.

TERRI: No.

RAY: "Amazing grace (that's God's unmerited favor, his mercy), how sweet the sound, that saved a wretch like me. I once was lost, but now I'm found, was blind, but now I see." That's the good news of the gospel. It's because God is rich in mercy and full of grace. He can grant us everlasting life as a free gift. We don't earn it by being good but by simply repenting and trusting in Christ, like you trust a parachute if you're going to jump out of a plane. It doesn't matter what you believe about gravity. It's going to kill you if you hit the ground at 120 miles an hour. So, fear causes you to put on a parachute. Your fear is your friend in that respect because it's causing you to see your danger.

Terri, I've tried to put the fear of God into you today because the fear of God is the beginning of wisdom. I tried to give you that extra information, hoping that you'll see fear as your friend, not your enemy—because it'll drive you to the mercy of God in Christ so your sins can be forgiven and so you can find everlasting life. You are so gracious and so kind to let me say all this without butting in. I know you probably haven't agreed with a lot of it, but you've been very kind to listen to me. Will you think about what we talked about?

I often ask people if they will think about our conversation. We know from the parable of the sower that the enemy tries to snatch the seed of the Word of God from the sinner's heart (see Mark 4:14–20). He won't be able to do that if they value what they've heard.

TERRI: Well, I know where you're coming from, and I hear it, and I don't know that I'm going to have a fear of God. But it'll make me think more about what you talked about.

RAY: That's wonderful. Can I give you a book that I've written?

TERRI: If it's not too big. I'm just walking. I'm exercising right now.

RAY: It's really small, and I'll give it to you now.

TERRI: All right.

RAY: [Hands her *How to Be Free from the Fear of Death*] Do you have a Bible at home?

TERRI: I do. I have several, actually.

RAY: Dust it off and check out what I'm saying, okay?

TERRI: All right, if I can find it. [Laughs]

RAY: Nice to talk to you.

What an unspeakable day of remorse it will be for so many on the day of judgment when they remember a Bible that sat in their home gathering dust for years. God gave us his Word as a lamp to our feet and a light to our path (see Psalm 119:105). Those who ignore it will reap the terrible consequences of their sins. If they only open a Bible, they will find that its divinely inspired pages tell us of a holy and just God, who is rich in mercy and is the source of all love—a love that was proved by his death in human form at the cross of Calvary. The Bible truly is the book of love.

CHAPTER 12

IDOLATRY DISTORTS GOD'S NATURE

Have you ever thought about the whistle of a bird? Go outside one morning with the determined attitude to put everything out of your mind and just listen to the birds. You will hear hundreds joyfully welcoming the morning. There is an orchestra of music. Then zero in on one. Listen to it sing. Think of the complexity of its song. Then think about how many millions of birds around the world are singing their own little hearts out with individual and complex tunes every morning. And we think we are insulting someone when we call them a birdbrain.

I love birds because they remind me of the greatness and power of God. How could he first think of and then have the mind to create flying creatures with their songs of such brilliant virtuosity, their wings, their eyes, their beating hearts, their amazing, individually styled feathers, their intuitive ability to create a nest for their offspring? They recognize their own kind and know how to flock together, stay clear of predators, search for their food, and land with such incredible agility that they make a pilot's perfect three-point landing look clumsy.

My wife, Sue, and I get to watch birds up close from the comfort of our living room. I put reflective film on the inside of one of the windows, then built a deck on the outside, onto which we put birdseed. Then we sit back and have a front seat into the world of wild birds—from colorful finches to crown sparrows, cooing doves, elegant California scrub jays, and, of course, regular sparrows.

Years ago, I also put up some wire netting and created an aviary for a number of cute and colorful little finches we purchased from the local pet shop. I often wondered if the caged birds ever wished that they could be as free as the wild birds, who had the liberty to fly into the vast blue heavens at will.

One day, as I was bird-watching, I was horrified to see a hawk swoop in, grab one of the terrified wild birds, and kill it as it screeched in terror. It was a horrible sight. When I ran outside, all I found were the feathered remnants of the attack. Tragically, the hawk had flown off with what was left of the bird in its claws.

An interesting reflection has come from seeing that shocking sight. I wonder if the birds in the caged environment (who would also have heard that awful sound) now see the cage as a place of safety.

Such is the way of the Christian home. Isn't it true that teenagers can sometimes feel trapped by the annoying boundaries their parents set for them? Don't these parents know that they are restricting their kids from the freedom to do what they want? Some of these teens may even feel their parents don't love them because they don't let them do whatever they please. But what many don't realize is that the hawks are waiting outside the cage.

As those teenagers mature and look back on life in the world, they will ultimately see some of those hawks take lives through alcoholism, drug addiction, suicide, and abortion. They will see the damage done by pornography, fornication, adultery, rape, bitterness, guilt, and much more. It's then that many will thank God for the love of their parents and those protective boundaries.

But the illustration goes deeper. Each of us, as Christians, is preserved in Christ, "having escaped the corruption that is in the world through lust" (2 Peter 1:4). Our Father has given us a cage to keep us from the enticement of sin. Out of his love for us, God forbid that we should ever gaze at the sinful pleasures of this world and long to be free from the confines of a life of cross-carrying and self-denial.

Robert was a confident, very strong-willed former drug addict. He had seen the evil of this world. Even though he had turned his life around through a rehabilitation program, Robert still didn't understand how a God of justice and protective boundaries could also be a God of love. Instead of believing in God, who so incredibly made the birds and all other living creatures, Robert made a god in his own image, which warped his view of God's true love.

RAY: Do you think there's an afterlife?

ROBERT: I know there's an afterlife. I've died many times. I've been resuscitated more times than you have fingers and toes. We don't actually die. We start right back at the same spot we are now until we reach that, I guess, Valhalla [In Norse mythology, Valhalla is a majestic, enormous hall located in Asgard, ruled over by the god Odin] or anything you want to call it. It will be a never-ending cycle until we perfect our own lives and ourselves.

No one has died many times. People do, however, have what are called near-death experiences. But they haven't died. They were *near* death. If you are near a place, you are not there yet. However, I didn't feel comfortable trying to correct him at this point as there was something a little unnerving about Robert. I fully expected him to become angry and walk off.

RAY: Do you believe in God's existence?

ROBERT: Absolutely. I believe I'm my own god, as everyone else is.

RAY: You are your own god?

ROBERT: Of course. God's not perfect.

RAY: God's not perfect?

ROBERT: Absolutely not. Even in the Bible he admits to there being other gods. He's a vengeful, jealous, and just God.

RAY: When you said even God admits to there being other gods, you're talking about the Ten Commandments. They begin with "I am the LORD your God…you shall have no other gods before Me" [Exodus 20:1, 3]. You know why he says that? Because man makes god in his own image. Hindus have 350 million gods. We have our own conception of God. We make up a god that's congenial to our sins. I did it before I was a Christian. It's called idolatry, and it's a transgression of the first of the Ten Commandments. The Bible says the God you have to face on judgment day *is* perfect. He's morally perfect. Are you doing anything that could be morally offensive to God? Are you a good person, or are you like the rest of us?

ROBERT: I'm righteous.

RAY: You're righteous?

ROBERT: I do what's right, not just for myself but for others, and it's basically keeping the moral compass pointed where it needs to.

RAY: Okay, so how many lies have you told in your life? That's the ninth commandment.

ROBERT: It's about as many grains of sand as there is here [points to the beach].

RAY: So, what do you call someone who tells lies?

ROBERT: I call him a liar.

RAY: So, what are you?

ROBERT: I'm a liar.

RAY: And you still think you're righteous?

ROBERT: Absolutely.

RAY: Have you ever stolen something?

ROBERT: Absolutely.

RAY: What do you call someone who steals?

ROBERT: A thief.

RAY: So, what are you?

ROBERT: I'm a thief.

RAY: No, you're not. You're a lying thief.

ROBERT: Yeah.

RAY: You still think you're a righteous person?

ROBERT: Yes, I do.

RAY: Have you ever used God's name in vain?

ROBERT: Of course.

RAY: Would you use your mother's name as a cuss word?

ROBERT: Absolutely.

RAY: You would? You've just broken the fifth commandment, which says, "Honor your father and mother." But most people would never do that, they wouldn't substitute their mother's name for [a cuss word] to express disgust, and yet that's what you've done with God's name, and it's holy. Godly Jews won't even speak his name because it's so holy.

ROBERT: Think about this, if Jesus died for our sins, right? What God would send any one of his children to an everlasting anything other than paradise or, you know, whatever it may be? If Jesus died for our sins, why would anyone go to hell?

This was a rabbit trail I wasn't going to follow. Robert wasn't showing any signs of reason or humility.

His body language was so stiff-necked I was surprised that I'd gotten as far as I had with him. I was convinced that he would become angry and walk off. I needed to take courage and give him more law to humble him.

> RAY: That's a really good question. Let's get back to it after we've looked at one more commandment. The last commandment we looked at was blasphemy, punishable by death in the Old Testament when you use God's name as a cuss word or fail to give it due honor. In the Sermon on the Mount, Jesus said, "Whoever looks upon a woman to lust for her has already committed adultery with her in his heart" [Matthew 5:28]. Have you ever looked at a woman with lust?
>
> ROBERT: Absolutely.
>
> RAY: Had sex before marriage?
>
> ROBERT: Absolutely.
>
> RAY: So, Robert, I'm not judging you; this is for you to judge yourself. You've told me that you're righteous, but at the same time you've told me you're a lying, thieving, blasphemous, fornicating, self-righteous adulterer at heart, and you have to face God on judgment day. If he judges you by those commandments, the Ten Commandments, I forgot the fifth

commandment, which is broken, are you going to be innocent or guilty?

ROBERT: Innocent.

This was frustrating but not unexpected. I decided to risk angering him with a gentle rebuke, but one that was done in the first person. I personalized Robert's philosophy to myself and then called myself deluded.

RAY: Robert, you'll be guilty like the rest of us. The Bible says there's not a righteous man on the face of the earth [Ecclesiastes 7:20], and the only way I could think myself to be righteous is if I had my own moral standard, which would be very low if I think it's righteous to be a lying, thieving, fornicating, blasphemous adulterer at heart, who dishonored his parents and broke the first commandment by having another god before him. If I thought I was righteous, I'd be deluded. You wouldn't be innocent on judgment day; you'd be guilty. So, if you're guilty, would you go to heaven or hell?

ROBERT: Neither.

RAY: Well, the Bible says that all liars will have their part in the lake of fire; no thief, no blasphemer, no adulterer, no fornicator, no idolater will inherit God's kingdom [see Revelation 21:8; 1 Corinthians 6:9–10]. So, Robert, you're up the river Niagara without a paddle. What can you do to justify yourself?

Let me share the gospel with you and see what you think. The Ten Commandments, that which we've looked at, are called the moral law. You and I broke the law. When Jesus was on the cross, he paid the fine. That's why he said, "It is finished," just before he died [John 19:30]. It is finished. In other words, the debt has been paid. Robert, if you're in court and someone pays your speeding fines, the judge can let you go. He can say, "This is serious, a lot of fines here, but someone's paid them. You're out of here." And he can do that which is legal and right and just. Well, God can legally dismiss your case. He can let you walk out of the courtroom. He can take the death sentence off you and save you from hell—all because Jesus paid the fine in his life's blood when he suffered for our sins. The Bible says, "Christ has once suffered for sins, the just for the unjust, that he might bring us to God" [1 Peter 3:18, author's paraphrase], and then he rose from the dead and defeated death.

Robert, if you'll just repent of your sins—stop saying, "I'm righteous; I'm innocent," and admit your sins—if you repent of those sins, turn from them, and trust in Jesus—not your own goodness but in Jesus—you've got a promise from the God who cannot lie that he'll remit your sins in an instant and grant you everlasting life. He'll give it to you as a free gift, not because you're good but because God is good and rich in mercy and kind to all those that call upon him.

ROBERT: You trust yourself to lift your own legs and walk?

RAY: Yes, sort of.

ROBERT: Do you believe in yourself?

RAY: No.

I was both surprised and encouraged that he hadn't become angry with me and walked away. Underneath a strong-willed, idolatrous, stubborn, self-righteous, and angry man was a heart that wanted to know. So I let him take control and ask me questions.

ROBERT: Why?

RAY: The Bible says, "He who trusts in his own heart is a fool" [Proverbs 28:26]. We're very fallible. We make mistakes. The person who put the eraser on the end of the pencil knew what he was doing because we're prone to error.

ROBERT: If you don't trust in your heart, listen to your heart, how will you ever find love?

RAY: I found love. I've been married for over fifty years. So, I follow my emotions, but I don't trust in my senses, especially not for my eternal salvation. Jesus said, "What will it profit a man if he gains the whole world, and loses his own soul?" [Mark 8:36]. You don't want to mess up your eternity, man. You can mess up things in this life. They're fixable, but if you die in your sins, it's not fixable. It's everlasting. It's damnation, and I don't want that to happen to you because I care about you.

ROBERT: I think to repent for anything that I've already forgiven myself for would involve, I guess, a paradox with the Bible because if Jesus died for our sins but we still have to repent for these sins to a father that would never send any one of his children to an everlasting inferno, I mean, what loving father would ever do that? If God's all-loving, why would he do that? And then to have to ask for forgiveness for something that's already been forgiven, that seems like an infallibility [sic]. It just seems like a paradox.

There was a different tone in Robert's voice. His bad theology had left him with a genuine dilemma. If God is all-loving, how could he create hell? It didn't make sense. My detection of the presence of humility encouraged me to address his idolatry.

RAY: That's a good question, but it's actually a straw man. Do you know what a straw man is?

ROBERT: What is that?

RAY: It's something you create that you can easily tear down. "God is all-loving" is a straw man. The Bible doesn't say God is all-loving anywhere. It says God is love, but he's not all-loving. That's like a criminal looking at a judge and saying, "The judge is all-loving; therefore, I'm just going to walk." No, if a judge is good, he's just and good. He'll make sure that justice is done. The Bible says God is love, but he's also righteous and holy, and you have to face him on judgment day.

He gave you a conscience, so you know right from wrong. Robert, listen to your conscience; acknowledge your sins. You've got a multitude of sins—you're just like the rest of us. I'm not pointing my finger at you. I'm just as sinful as you. I need a Savior more than I need the air that I breathe—and so do you if you want to keep that precious life of yours. You've had a hard life. You're in recovery, and things are better. You're enjoying life. You don't want to lose it. Man, you don't want to lose it. Jesus said, "He that seeks to save his life will lose it, but he that loses his life, for my sake, shall save it" [Matthew 16:25, author paraphrase]. So, lose yourself in Christ; repent and trust in Jesus. Do you have a Bible at home?

ROBERT: No, I do not.

RAY: Can I give you a book that I've written?

ROBERT: I would respectfully decline.

RAY: Can I show it to you?

ROBERT: Respectfully decline.

RAY: I'm going to show it to you anyway.

ROBERT: All right.

RAY: [Gives Robert *How to Be Free from the Fear of Death*]

I'm a bulldog when it comes to getting this book into the hands of someone who has just heard the gospel. This is because I know that every time Robert glances at it (even if it's not open), it will remind him of our conversation.

ROBERT: Thank you.

RAY: So, you're going to take it?

ROBERT: I will accept it.

RAY: I really appreciate it. Great to talk to you, Robert.

ROBERT: Thank you.

His "I will accept it" was huge for me because, for the entire conversation, I was wondering what was going on with this man. His initial refusal of the book told me that he was letting me come so far but no farther. A wrong view of God is a road sign that sends sinners in the wrong direction. If God isn't holy, he doesn't care about evil. There is, therefore, no hell, and the cross is irrelevant.

CHAPTER 13

SIN AND RESPONSIBILITY

It's often wise to ask a sinner who they think Jesus was. Was he just a man? Most have no idea that the Bible tells us that he was God manifest in the flesh—the express image of the invisible God. Their reaction will also show you if they respect his words. If they believe in another version of Jesus, it's going to be an uphill battle. They may think that everything Jesus said about sin, righteousness, and judgment can be discarded. But our confidence as Christians isn't in our eloquent words. With the help of the Holy Spirit, in the power of the gospel, and in the faithfulness of God to watch over his Word, we can have confidence that Jesus is who he said he is and that sin, righteousness, and judgment exist as he described.

Carlisa was one of those people who had her own ideas about who Jesus is and how he feels about sin. She was as proud as a peacock, and talking to her was challenging right from the get-go.

> RAY: Do you believe the Bible?
>
> CARLISA: I don't believe in organized religion.
>
> RAY: Jesus didn't believe in organized religion. Organized religion killed him; they killed all the prophets. Have you ever studied what Jesus said about life and death?
>
> CARLISA: Yeshua?
>
> RAY: Yes, Jesus.
>
> CARLISA: Put some respect on this man's name.

She laughed at and showed contempt for the precious name of Jesus. In recent years it's become trendy to use Jesus' Hebrew name instead of his English name. But it makes sense to use the English language when we are speaking of Jesus to English-speaking people because unbelievers (those we're trying to reach) will have no idea whom we're talking about if we refer to him in a foreign language they neither speak nor understand. We may as well be saying, "Put your faith in *Иисус Христос* (Jesus Christ in Russian)" to people who don't know the Russian language. When I have mentioned this, many responses show they despise the name of Jesus with a passion, which is really why they refuse to use it.

I was once preaching the gospel in the open air at the University of California, Berkeley, and was being angrily heckled by a man who was obviously demon possessed. He hated it when I used the name of Jesus and insisted that I call him Yeshua. He knew that my hearers wouldn't have any idea of whom I was speaking if I used a foreign language. The name of Jesus is so hated by this world that it's used in place of a cuss word. Ask yourself why Jesus is used in such a horrible way and why the name Yeshua isn't.

> CARLISA: He was a very advanced being, and he believed in reincarnation too.
>
> RAY: I'm talking about the Jesus of the Bible, the one who said this...
>
> CARLISA: I don't know that guy.

The Bible says that we don't wrestle with human beings but with demons (see Ephesians 6:12–20), and I sure felt of that battle with Carlisa. So I decided to do what Jesus did when he was face-to-face with the devil. He quoted the Word of God (see Matthew 4:3–4).

> RAY: Well, I'll share his words with you. He said, "Love your enemies; do good to those that despitefully use you" [Matthew 5:44, author's paraphrase]. He said, "If your eye offends you pluck it out, for it's better to enter heaven

without an eye than go to hell with both your eyes" [Matthew 18:9, author's paraphrase]. He said, "Marvel not at this, for the hour is coming when all that are in the grave shall hear my voice" [John 5:28, author's paraphrase]. He said, "I'm the resurrection and the life. He who believes in me, though he dies, yet shall he live, and whoever lives and believes in me shall never die" [John 11:25–26, author's paraphrase].

Never a man spoke like this man, and his words were unique—because the Bible says he was God in human form, the express image of the invisible God. So, I've got a big question for you; do you think you're a good person?

CARLISA: I do good things; sometimes I don't do good things. I'm learning every day.

RAY: So, how are you going to do on judgment day?

CARLISA: I judge myself. It's not about anything else.

RAY: Well, you've got an appointment to keep. The Bible says it's appointed to man once to die and after this the judgment [see Hebrews 9:27]. God's got an appointment for you; let's see how you're going to do on judgment day. Can you be honest with me?

CARLISA: Of course. That's all there is at the end of the day. I mean, my higher power loves me regardless. I'm the one who's judging myself.

RAY: How many lies have you told in your life?

CARLISA: I couldn't count.

RAY: Have you ever stolen something?

CARLISA: Of course.

RAY: Have you ever used God's name in vain?

CARLISA: Absolutely.

RAY: Do you love your mom?

CARLISA: Yes.

RAY: Would you ever use her name as a cuss word?

CARLISA: If I had to, in the moment…sure.

RAY: Really? That's a violation of the fifth commandment: "Honor your father and mother." Most people would never use their mother's name as a cuss word, but you've taken the holy name of *God*—a name that godly Jews won't even speak it is so holy; they won't even write it down—and used it in the place of [a cuss] word to express disgust. It's called blasphemy, very serious in God's eyes. I appreciate your honesty. Jesus said that if you look with lust, you commit adultery in the heart [see Matthew 5:28]. Have you ever looked with lust?

CARLISA: Oh yes.

RAY: This is for you to judge yourself to see how you'll do on judgment day. You've told me you're a lying thief, a blasphemer, and an adulterer at heart. So, if God judges you by those Ten Commandments on judgment day, will you be innocent or guilty?

CARLISA: Innocent.

Underneath every witnessing encounter, there is the immutable biblical truth that people love darkness rather than light because their deeds are evil (see John 3:19). That's why idolatry is embraced with both hands. The Bible doesn't say that sinners are attracted to sin. It says that they love it! So they are going to desperately hold on to that idol because it proclaims them innocent, which eliminates, in their minds, any problems with guilt, an angry God, moral responsibility, judgment day, and hell. Their devotion to idolatry is the ultimate delusion.

RAY: Why?

CARLISA: Because I was honest.

RAY: Well, it's like saying to a judge, "I committed the crime but I'm innocent because I was honest." The judges will say, "You should be honest. This is a court of law." No, you'll be guilty like the rest of us.

CARLISA: No…you're referring to man's law; we're talking about God's law here.

RAY: God's law is far higher.

CARLISA: No, there's a misunderstanding here. Men try to interpret God based upon their limited understanding. This is beyond what common man can even comprehend. Unconditional love is not based on adultery, lust, or sin. We're in human vehicles. We're in these bodies in order to enjoy, experience. We don't always know what's right or wrong. We have some sensations, temptations, and we go through that. So, if I make one mistake, I'm gonna go to hell? Of course not.

RAY: Do you know what you've just done? You just broken the first and the second of the Ten Commandments. Do you know what they are? Number one is "I am the Lord your God; you shall have no other gods before me." And the second commandment says, "Don't make up a false God," and you can do it with your mind. I did it before I was a Christian. You create a snuggly, cuddly god you feel happy with—a god that has no sense of justice or truth or righteousness. A god that's so loving he doesn't care that a woman is raped and murdered. Although what Hitler did was bad, he just couldn't care less.

But the God of the Bible said there's going to be a day of judgment, and it's a fearful thing to fall into his hands. But he's so rich in mercy, he doesn't take any pleasure in the death of the wicked [see Ezekiel 33:11]. He provided a Savior in Christ. Do you know that? God provided a Savior to save you from death. Christ died for the sin of the world.

CARLISA: No, he didn't. He died for his own sins. We're all responsible for our own sins. We all carry our own cross. Jesus was an example that's all, an example of someone overcoming their trials and tribulations, and we have that same responsibility ourselves. You can't say, "Oh, Jesus died for my sins." No, he didn't…so if you go and just shoot someone in the head right now, and you say, "Well, Jesus died for my sins two thousand years ago. I'm redeemed. I'm okay."

RAY: That's playing the hypocrite. They're going to end up in hell. [Their sin is] wrong; you know that.

CARLISA: No, but at the end of the day, that's the whole concept of Christianity. It's like I'm not taking accountability for myself. Yes, you should.

RAY: Is you're family Christian?

CARLISA: I *do* have family that's Christian.

RAY: They're praying for you. You're a prodigal. They want you back. They want you right with God; they want to see you in heaven, and so do I. So, think about your upbringing. Think about Christ on the cross.

The night I became a Christian, I heard that my wife's family had been praying for my salvation. That moved me. It spoke to me of their love. That's why I regularly tell young people that their Christian parents are no doubt praying for their salvation. This is not only a reminder of their parental love but also a reminder of the necessity for God to draw rebellious sinners to himself. It's not within us to come to the light without his enabling help.

CARLISA: They're drunk off religion…they're drunk on this high that they can be redeemed by this Christian God, you know, and I'm not someone who hates religion. I think it's a good starting point, but you have to move beyond that as you mature your soul, so what you're talking about is elementary, and if you're talking to an audience who have no concept of God, keep doing this work. But if you're trying to reach people who are trying to change the world truly, you need to up your understanding.

In other words, she was offended by the simplicity of the gospel—what the Bible calls the "offense of the cross" (Galatians 5:11). This has a logical explanation. If I offered you a parachute on a plane, but you believed you didn't have to jump, the parachute would be irrelevant. If you were enjoying a good meal and intently watching a movie on the flight, my insistence that you put it on would be an annoyance.

What Carlisa didn't realize was that God has deliberately kept it simple so that the humble will hear the gospel and the proud would be offended by the simplicity.

RAY: Jesus said, "Unless you become as a little child, you're not entering God's kingdom" [Matthew 18:3, author's paraphrase]. That's the wisdom of God. This is what he said: "I thank you, O Father, you have hid these things from the wise and prudent and revealed them to babes" [Matthew 11:25, author's paraphrase]. So, humble yourself, seek after God because death could seize upon you tonight, and if you died in your sins it would grieve my heart... grieve your family's heart. So, dust that old Bible off and say, "God, I've sinned against you. I need a Savior. I need to be washed."

CARLISA: I have not sinned against God.

RAY: Oh, you told me you're a lying, thieving, blasphemous adulterer at heart.

CARLISA: Sin doesn't even exist. It's a concept made up by man.

Earlier she said, "We're all responsible for our own sins." Watch how illogical and even foolish it is to deny the reality of sin.

RAY: It's another word for "evil." Do you think evil exists?

CARLISA: No.

RAY: Is rape evil?

CARLISA: It kills the soul.

RAY: It's evil.

CARLISA: It kills the soul.

RAY: Is pedophilia evil?

CARLISA: Yes; it kills the soul of the child.

RAY: Was Hitler evil?

CARLISA: That's debatable.

RAY: So, you can't even answer a question like that. Eleven million people slaughtered by him, and you won't even say he's evil? You know why? When you've got no moral absolutes, you're like a ship without a rudder. You can't even say something is evil. You don't even say rape is evil. Hitler was evil. God says we're all evil. He called his disciples evil. He said, "If you [then], being evil, know how to give good gifts to your children" [Matthew 7:11]. God's standard is infinitely higher than yours and mine, and that's the standard he's going to judge us with on judgment day—and you need a Savior. We care about you. We love you. We want to see you in heaven.

CARLISA: This conversation is interesting. I love it, but I just don't feel that this is relevant to what's going on in today's society.

This was evidence of her love for this sinful world. She didn't have the time or the inclination to trust in God's mercy. The cross was irrelevant to her.

RAY: Well, death is relevant…it's coming. You don't know when it's going to come.

CARLISA: The body…the spiritual being that God created never dies. It's energy. All it does is transform. That's it. The body...you are not a body; you're not a mind.

RAY: Where do you get this from?

CARLISA: This is from higher knowledge, the real God, the God who you don't know yet but whom you're on the way to learning.

RAY: You made it up.

CARLISA: No.

RAY: Where did you get this knowledge?

CARLISA: Meditation, seeking the truth of God, the Creator of all, the one that I respect and love beyond anything. Your projection of where I'm at in my spiritual journey—I love it because you're challenging me. And I love to be challenged because you're showing me a part of myself I'm not comfortable with yet. I've got some work to do. Thank you.

RAY: Can I give you a book that I wrote?

CARLISA: Oh, yeah, sure. What's it called?

RAY: It's called *How to Be Free from the Fear of Death*.

CARLISA: Listen, death is nothing more than a transformation. I used to live next to a cemetery. It was the most peaceful place I've ever been.

RAY: Because they're all dead in there, that's why.

CARLISA: At the end of the day, death is just a transformation.

RAY: It's wages.

CARLISA: And you go and take on a new body in this realm if you'd like to, or you can go to another dimension if you're done with earth, if you've learned your lessons, and you've broken the cycle of reincarnation, which this is trying to entrap souls. So, you better be careful of what you're doing to God.

RAY: Are you going think about what we talked about?

CARLISA: No.

RAY: But it's [worth more than] a hundred million dollars. [Gives her the *Million Dollar Gospel of John*]

CARLISA: Oh my goodness.

RAY: It's the Gospel of John.

CARLISA: Oh wow, well, thank you so much…

Our conversation wasn't enjoyable. Some are a delight, and the determining factor is humility. But love doesn't give up on the proudest of souls. Jesus didn't give up on me, so how could I give up on Carlisa?

There is a temptation to think to ourselves, when someone rejects the gospel, *You are going to regret this on the day of judgment.* But thinking we will say, "I told you so," on that day isn't something we can take consolation in. The stakes are too high. This is the precious life of a human being. Instead of spending our energies on thinking such thoughts, we should get on our knees for them, praying that God removes the blinders from those who don't fear him or understand the consequences of sin.

CHAPTER 14

A FORMER MORMON'S TESTIMONY

I was filming on the pier at Huntington Beach one Saturday when I was approached by a couple who said that they loved our ministry and that the man, John, had come out of Mormonism. When I asked him if he would come on camera, he was more than willing. In this chapter, John will be doing most of the talking because what he said was so informative, although there are a couple of brief transcripts from other occasions when I talked to members of the Church of Jesus Christ of Latter-day Saints (LDS) and some comments from Mormon sources to authenticate John's experience.

> RAY: You were raised LDS, and you're now a Christian?
>
> JOHN: Yes, sir.
>
> RAY: So, what happened?

JOHN: Well, a whole lot in between. So, I mean, growing up in the LDS Church never really landed. That was a time of tension in the family because it's an expectation that you go.

RAY: On a mission.

JOHN: Yes, that's right. Every young man when he's nineteen has to go for two years.

Perhaps you have experienced young men who have gone door-to-door in your neighborhood to convert people to the Church of Jesus Christ of Latter-day Saints.

RAY: What is that for? What do they achieve?

JOHN: Well, it is to proselyte, as it were, and to spread their version of the gospel, which really is not the gospel at all. It's the laws and ordinances of the LDS Church and for a long time was the fastest growing religion in the world. I don't know that to be true anymore, but it's the expectation for every young man to go. So I did not go.

RAY: Is the salvation dependent on whether they do that or not?

JOHN: Yes, that and one of their Articles of Faith says all men are saved through Christ but also by obedience and laws and ordinances of the gospel. So, I understood the gospel to mean the laws and the ordinances of the LDS Church. Not only can we not keep the law that's written in our heart and that's written in the Bible, but you have additional ordinances in the LDS Church. So, you can never keep up with it. There is never assurance. You never really land.

RAY: It is by grace you are saved *after all that you can do.*

JOHN: That's right.

RAY: That leaves an open end, and it's kind of scary. I've talked to many LDS people, and I say, "You'll go to heaven?" They say, "I hope so."

Through my years of sharing the gospel, many of the Mormons I have encountered have a works-based mentality where salvation is dependent on obedience, which produces an uncertainty about their status with God. See what this man in another encounter had to say when asked about his salvation:

MORMON 1: How can you say that I am saved just by grace alone? It is through your service, through your sacrifice, and through doing everything you can to make your own Father proud, that he's going to say, "Okay, my good and faithful servant, welcome home."

RAY: Listen to God's Word, and I'll say it slowly. Scripture says, "For by grace are you saved through faith, *and that not of yourselves*; it's the gift of God, not of works, lest any man boasts" [Ephesians 2:8–9, author's paraphrase and emphasis].

MORMON 1: Heavenly Father is not just going to give us gifts if we're not going to do anything to show him that we're doing everything we can to make him proud. You don't get something for nothing. Ever.

In another conversation with two young Mormons, they both expressed uncertainty about where they will go in the afterlife, but I could hear from their tone that they wanted assurance, assurance they couldn't find in Mormonism.

RAY: When you die, where will you go?

MORMON 2: It depends on how you acted and, you know, if you repented for sins or anything like that.

RAY: Where are you going to go?

MORMON 2: I don't know.

RAY: You don't know?

MORMON 2: I wish I knew.

RAY: Could you end up in outer darkness, in hell?

MORMON 2: I could.

RAY: Does that concern you?

MORMON 2: Yes, it would suck. I can't say I'd be happy about going there.

RAY: What about you?

MORMON 3: I hope I don't go to outer darkness.

How freeing it is to believe Jesus paid the debt for our sins! Those who believe and repent can have assurance that they will spend eternity with Jesus because we are saved by Christ alone. Returning to my conversation with John, I asked him about how the Christian's assurance of salvation differs from LDS beliefs.

RAY: So what's the difference? I mean, the knowledge you have as a born-again Christian and what you have as an LDS?

JOHN: Well, it's just that…it's the assurance factor. Now we want to grow into our obedience of the Lord, but it is more out of a love for him and a reverent fear than a fear that you can't make the cut, that there's a 60 percent grade, maybe a 65 percent, whatever the cutoff is. It's like, you know, if I'd been caught in a bad day and the Lord chose to take me back on that day, well, then I'd be headed for hell. But there really is no hell, either, in the LDS Church.

RAY: Yes, outer darkness.

JOHN: Outer darkness. You know, there are very few, they don't call them mortal sins, but it is that you have your mortal sins. There are very few that really go to hell otherwise. There are different tiers of heaven in which you can work out your salvation and sort of ascend and the ultimate goal of kind of becoming a god yourself.

Latter-day Saints have several beliefs about heaven and hell that differ from what the Bible says. Here is a conversation among a few Mormons about their view of hell and different layers of heaven.

MORMON 4: To define what hell is within the Mormon belief, that's a really tough thing to do. Often times it takes some critical reading skills to figure out what the Scriptures mean when they're talking about hell. There's no fire there, and our view of heaven is so radically different than any other religion.

MORMON 5: When Latter-day Saints talk about heaven, it's done in two ways. One heaven is where you're going in the afterlife. Whether it's the lowest layer of heaven or the highest, it's heaven.

MORMON 6: Next layer of heaven that we believe in, in the LDS Church, is the terrestrial kingdom, and this kingdom is for people who had the chance to partake of the gospel but then just chose not to.

MORMON 4: The coveted celestial kingdom, which is where we all want to go, terrestrial kingdom, and then the next one is called the telestial kingdom, and if you're wondering where, I mean I'm not the judge, but if you're wondering where Hitler probably went, it's probably that one. When we talk about hell and who goes to hell, I mean, in one sense, all three of these kingdoms or levels of heaven are still better than where we're at right now.

Although many Mormons would call themselves Christians, even these brief conversations reveal undeniable differences, differences that contradict the truth of the Bible. Based on John's experiences growing up LDS, I wanted to see how he would advise Bible-believing Christians to witness to members of the LDS Church.

RAY: How would you witness to an LDS?

JOHN: Just the true gospel, really, which is that there's an irreconcilable gap between us and a holy God, and just what the cross accomplished was namely closing that gap. So there's very little understanding of what that means. The LDS don't use the cross as a symbol because they see it as a symbol of death, and that's how we're brought to life, through the blood of Christ.

The symbol Christians see as a sign of victory over death, Jesus' love, and fulfilled prophecies is what Mormons see only as a sign of death. Read how two Mormons discuss the cross:

MORMON 5: Why don't we parade around crosses everywhere? Well, the simple reason is, and Gordon B. Hinckley [fifteenth president of LDS Church] says something about this, we believe that the symbol of Christ is his teachings. We don't want to give Christ just one little symbol. Especially not this, what he was murdered on. The symbol of eternal life should not be the death of the Savior.

MORMON 7: I've always been uncomfortable with that idea, that the thing that we use to remind ourselves is one of the most tragic events in history of the universe.

In their statements, these Mormons reveal a lack of understanding about the true significance of the cross. While Jesus did die on the cross, he rose again. The cross was not merely a place of defeat but rather the means through which we can experience eternal life with our Creator.

JOHN: It's interesting that they refuse to use that symbol, because, again, it's not about Christ's defeat. That was his defeat *over* death. What that means to us is that we have defeat over death and defeat over sin. But they don't use that symbol because it means something different to them.

They have their own set of works in the scriptures—many who will hear this will be familiar with the quad scriptures. What is that? Well, it's the Holy Bible, the Book of Mormon, Doctrine and Covenants, and Pearl of Great Price, and as a child even, I had this sense of that first half of the quad being the Holy Bible was sort of that thing in the beginning that you skipped over to get to First Nephi and then you read from there.

So there is little understanding of the Holy Bible, at least from my standpoint as a child and as an adolescent. Maybe some Old Testament stories stuck, but the Gospels were not really something that landed or were taught and definitely not the Epistles and so much more in Scripture, and there's a reason for that.

It's there, but we don't study it. We study the Book of Mormon, and we touch base on some Old Testament stories and so forth.

RAY: They don't want to use the word *Mormon* anymore. Is that correct?

JOHN: I think they kind of embraced it...this has been interesting too. Just as observation over the last fifteen years or so where they really leaned on marketing and wanted to soften themselves to the world. That's one example. They had the "I'm a Mormon" campaign. They started to have marketing campaigns and softening their message, how we are to present it. For instance, at one point, we were coached to not say that we believe this is the only true church anymore.

Although adherence to the belief that the LDS Church is the only true church has decreased in recent years, *Mormon Doctrine*, an encyclopedic analysis of the LDS Church's doctrine, states, "If it had not been for Joseph Smith and the restoration, there would be no salvation. There is no salvation outside The Church of Jesus Christ of Latter-day Saints."[16]

JOHN: I found that to be really interesting and how they would answer not giving Black people the keys to the Melchizedek priesthood, which is an honor to have in the Mormon Church. We were just basically not to address that point because we didn't need to. But what I think you're seeing is a falling away from that faith because there is no rod on which to grab. There's no solid footing; there's no traction. So, people are falling away from that and going to the gospel, which is true—and *it* is a rod and staff that comforts us.

RAY: So, what brought you to Christ?

JOHN: After leaving the LDS Church, and this is when I was a teenager, I wanted nothing to do with Christianity because that's what I thought it was. I wanted nothing to do with religion. I was fairly well-reasoned as to why it was. I was very intellectually atheistic in all this. And then, I don't know...there's just a tipping point and a kind of slow progression. I think a lot of people have this defining moment, a saving moment. I don't know that I had that or not, but one thing is for sure is that I'm born again, and I love Christ, and I seek the Word and seek to learn and grow in it all the time.

RAY: So you came to a knowledge of sin, and the cross made sense once you understood you were a sinner.

JOHN: Yes, exactly! That's a great way of putting it. Once I understood what the cross meant and what it represented, closing the gap between a holy God who can't accept sin and that we have a sinful nature, which is something that the LDS also rejects. It's in their Articles of Faith as well that we are punished according to our own sins and not for Adam's transgression. It is attractive for some because it denies original sin. "We don't have a sin nature." It's all about what we do, but if it is about all we do, then we're in trouble.

RAY [TO JOHN'S WIFE]: Can you come on camera?

JOHN'S WIFE: Yes.

RAY: Jump in.

RAY: So this is your wonderful wife.

JOHN: Yes, it is.

JOHN'S WIFE: Just something I noticed in his life, because I was raised Christian, but watching him, he would say for a while, he didn't know where to hang his hat. But I remember when you did know that you were going to hang your hat on Jesus Christ as your Lord and Savior. He was listening to a lot of R. C. Sproul, and he was like "Wow! The Bible is inerrant and infallible and the Word of God, and I can trust it." That,

I feel, is where the tipping point was because the LDS, or the Mormons, they believe that the Bible is true as far as it is translated correctly.

Many Mormons don't trust the Bible because the books were originally written in languages other than English. Look how author and former dean at Brigham Young University Andrew Skinner discussed how *The Doctrine and Covenants*, a book Mormons believe to be divine revelations, is more trustworthy than the Bible:

> New Testament first composed in a language other than English, composed maybe, we don't know, but some books maybe in Aramaic. Certainly, all of the books in Greek, Old Testament first composed in Hebrew... *The Doctrine and Covenants* is unique in that is our only volume of the standard works that was revealed in the first instance in the English language. It was revealed in the language of Joseph Smith, which...his mother tongue was the English language. So, there is no opportunity... for mistranslation. This came straight from the Lord to the Lord's prophet, and...that makes it an incredible book, an exciting book of scripture to look at.[17]

The Christian embraces the Bible as God's Word because it's self-evident. It is filled with amazing prophecies and is uniquely and consistently wise about every walk of life. It reveals the uniqueness of Jesus and his incredible words. These things show us that it is divinely inspired. However, our confidence in the Scriptures comes back to simple faith. We trust that God (without a doubt) has preserved his Word.

RAY: So you had faith in God's Word, and then the gospel made sense to you?

JOHN: Exactly.

JOHN'S WIFE: They [Mormons] don't like being told that they're not Christian though. I've noticed that's offensive to them.

JOHN: There are irreconcilable differences there, and then I've observed, too, just not in my own family but in many that I love, there's a low level of discernment amongst LDS people. In other words, it's easy for them to get caught up in outward things, not just works but the way they present themselves from an outward way and how the enemy will seep in and grab them. So, whether it's just through occultic things and stories and books and other media and things like that, I think there's a low-level discernment because really they don't have the true Holy Spirit protecting and dwelling in them.

And I don't say this with any relish at all. It really saddens me because I have a deep affection, like I said, not only for my family, many of whom are LDS, but for the LDS people. If I could say anything to reach out to them, it would just be to trust in Christ and in Christ alone and in his Word.

Tipping point, I think that's when I started to trust the Word as inerrant, which wasn't just, you know, an act of decision to trust. It was the more I read it, it just revealed itself to me, and it was this ever-unfurling red carpet, a beautiful thing. So, as soon as I started to be able to trust in the Word and hold on to it, that's when I started to be regenerated and really became born again from that.

In his response, John's testimony expresses the life-changing nature of the true gospel. The Bible both reveals the truth about our sin and the reality that Jesus' death on the cross paid for our sins, closing the gap between humanity and God with an act of grace. The cross represents the fact that we don't have to earn our salvation. Jesus paid it all.

CHAPTER 15

MORE THAN MISTAKES

Damian was a backslidden Mormon. As you will see, he, like many others, tried to console himself with the law. One of the greatest revelations we can have is that the law cannot help us with our sin problem. All it does is condemn. It points its holy finger at us and accuses us of sin. Its function is like that of a mirror. A mirror just reveals what you are in truth. It shows us where we need to wash. In our right minds, we wouldn't try to wash ourselves with a mirror. Its function is to send us to the water. And so it is with God's law. It reflects that we are unclean in his sight and sends us to the fount of mercy, where we can be washed.

RAY: Tell me your thoughts on the afterlife.

DAMIAN: You can either grow up in heaven or hell, depending on whatever you believe in.

RAY: You're talking about life before we were born, is that what you're saying?

DAMIAN: Life before we're born, correct.

RAY: So, this is a Mormon doctrine?

DAMIAN: Yes.

RAY: Have you been born again?

DAMIAN: Honestly, I don't know. I think so.

RAY: You're not sure?

DAMIAN: I'm not sure.

RAY: You know in John chapter 3, Jesus said, "Except a man be born again, he cannot see the kingdom of God" [v. 3, author's paraphrase]. So, it's essential you're born again. He said, "Marvel not that I say you must be born again" [v. 7, author's paraphrase]. I've got a question for you—who was Judas?

This was a strange question to ask, but I was preparing a teaching for our YouTube channel where I said that we could learn much from Judas. His life was a great example of what *not* to do. The first lesson was to beware of the subtlety of covetousness. Judas loved money, and it deceived him. I thought that Damian would, of course, know who Judas was.

DAMIAN: Judas? I know who Mary is. I do not know who Judas is.

RAY: He was the one that betrayed Jesus.

DAMIAN: The fallen angel?

RAY: No, that was Lucifer.

DAMIAN: Lucifer, okay.

RAY: When did you last read your Bible?

DAMIAN: It's been a good minute, a good few months. Probably back in June, July.

RAY: Judas was the one that betrayed Jesus; he was one of the disciples. The Bible says he was stealing money. He was the treasurer, but he was stealing money from the bag…he was a hypocrite. Are you going to make it to heaven?

DAMIAN: I believe I will.

RAY: Why?

DAMIAN: By doing the right thing and staying away from all the negative things around you. Staying positive with a good, great mind and always talking to God is always the way to do it and always the way to go. It'll keep your mind clear and your mind on the right path to success.

RAY: So, is that what Mormonism has taught you?

DAMIAN: Yes, sir.

RAY: Are you a good person?

DAMIAN: Yes, I'm a good person. I'm nice, I share, I give to the poor.

RAY: Are you morally good?

DAMIAN: Yes, I'd say that.

RAY: Okay, I'm going to give you a standard to judge yourself, and then you make a judgment after we've looked at the standard. The standard is the Ten Commandments. You're familiar with them?

DAMIAN: Yes.

RAY: Let's go to the ninth: "You shall not be a false witness." How many lies have you told in your life?

DAMIAN: I told a few.

RAY: Have you ever stolen something?

DAMIAN: No, sir.

RAY: Have you ever used God's name in vain?

DAMIAN: Yes, sir.

RAY: Would you use your mother's name as a cuss word? You hit your thumb with a hammer, and you want to express how you feel, so you could use [a filth] word to express disgust or her name in its place. You'd equate the two. Would you do that with your mother's name?

DAMIAN: No, sir.

RAY: Why not?

DAMIAN: Because I don't know…that's my mom.

RAY: You respect her?

DAMIAN: Yes, sir.

RAY: But you have done that with God's name, the one who gave you a mother, the one who gave you life, and his name is holy. Damian, that's called blasphemy. It's so serious in the Old Testament that it's punishable by death. Do you still think you're a good person?

DAMIAN: No, sir.

RAY: Once again, I appreciate your honesty. Jesus said, "Whoever looks at a woman and lusts for her has already committed adultery with her in his heart" [Matthew 5:28, author paraphrase]. Have you ever looked at a woman with lust?

DAMIAN: No, sir, except the girl that I'm with now, currently.

RAY: You have looked with lust then?

DAMIAN: Yes, sir.

RAY: This is for you to judge yourself. I'm not judging you because we've just met, but you've told me you're a liar, a blasphemer, and an adulterer at heart. Have you had sex before marriage?

DAMIAN: Yes, sir.

RAY: And a fornicator. So, if God judges you by the Ten Commandments (we've looked at four of them) on judgment day, are you going to be innocent or guilty?

DAMIAN: I'd be guilty.

RAY: Heaven or hell?

DAMIAN: Probably most likely hell.

RAY: Now, does that concern you?

DAMIAN: A little bit, but you know, I could always do better. You learn from your mistakes.

The word *mistakes* can be telling. Sometimes it can mean that people see their sins (in that they made a mistake in choosing to sin) or that their sin was just a mistake rather than being evil. More often than not, it reveals that they don't see the gravity of their sin.

RAY: Do you know repentance can't help you in that case? Do you know why?

DAMIAN: No, I don't.

RAY: Well, imagine yourself being in a court of law and you've broken the law and it's a very serious crime. Let's say you've robbed a bank and shot a guard, and he died. Very serious. The judge says you're guilty, and you say, "I *am* guilty, but I want to tell you, judge, I'm very sorry, and I'll never do it again."

DAMIAN: [Laughs] You're going to get nowhere with it.

RAY: Yes, he's going to say, "Of course you should be sorry. Of course you shouldn't do it again. You're going to jail," and it's the same with God. We can say we're sorry, we'll never do it again, which is what repentance is, but of course we should be sorry, and of course we shouldn't do it again. So, repentance by itself can't save us. Do you know what can save you from hell?

DAMIAN: No, sir.

RAY: You have no idea?

DAMIAN: Other than praying to God and just make sure you don't break none of the commandments.

Damian still thought the law that condemns him can help him. It can't. He was in debt to the law—it called for his blood.

RAY: Too late, they're already broken.

DAMIAN: Yes, sir.

RAY: You know, it's like saying to the judge, "I think I can talk to you some more, and I won't break the law again," and he'll say, "Good, you're going to jail." You need something else. Didn't they tell you in the Mormon Church?

DAMIAN: No, sir.

RAY: You need God's mercy.

DAMIAN: [Nods] God's mercy.

RAY: That's what you do if you're in a court of law, and you're guilty, and you can't justify yourself. You throw yourself on the mercy of the judge. The Bible says, "God is rich in mercy to all that call upon him" [Psalm 86:5, author's paraphrase]. Do you know why God can forgive you in an instant?

DAMIAN: I kind of have an idea, but I'm not really sure.

RAY: Jesus died on the cross for the sin of the world.

DAMIAN: That's what I was going to say.

RAY: Yes, we broke God's law, the Ten Commandments. Jesus paid the fine. That's why he said, "It is finished," just before he died [John 19:30]. Do you remember he said that? It is finished. He was saying that the debt had been paid.

If you're in court and someone pays your fine, even though you're guilty, a judge can let you go. He can say, "Damian, there's a stack of speeding fines here, but someone's paid them. You're out of here." He can do that which is legal and right and just…even though you're guilty, you walk because someone paid your fine. And even though you and I are guilty before God of heinous crimes in his eyes, he can forgive us in an instant, let us walk out of his courtroom because Jesus paid the fine on the cross in full. The Bible says, "Christ has once suffered for sins, the just for the unjust, that he might bring us to God" [1 Peter 3:18, author's paraphrase]. So, you and I can live forever. Death can be taken off us all because of the death and resurrection of the Savior.

And what you must do, and this is the essential point, is repent of your sins. Yes, you say, "God, I'm sorry. I've used your name as a cuss word. I've lied. I've looked with lust, had sex out of marriage, and I've sinned against you, but please forgive me. I'm truly sorry." That's genuine repentance—and then you trust in Jesus like you trust a parachute. If you're going to jump out of a plane, why would you put on a parachute?

DAMIAN: So it could save your life.

RAY: Yes, and the motivation would be fear. You don't want to hit the ground at 120 miles an hour.

DAMIAN: No, sir.

RAY: So, fear, in that respect, is good because it's driving you to the parachute. Damian, what I've tried to do with you is put the fear of God in you ("The fear of God is the beginning of wisdom," the Bible says [Proverbs 9:10, author's paraphrase]), hoping you'll see that fear is your friend, not your enemy.

DAMIAN: [Nods] Okay.

RAY: You're in big trouble; you need a Savior. You need to put the parachute on. You need to trust in Jesus and not your goodness. Can you hear what I'm saying?

DAMIAN: Yes, sir.

RAY: Is it making sense?

DAMIAN: Makes a lot of sense.

RAY: Are you going to think about what we talked about?

DAMIAN: Of course. I think I should.

RAY: When are you going to repent and trust alone in Christ?

DAMIAN: Whenever I get the chance to be alone, whenever I could.

RAY: Why not now? Who says you're going to get home? You've got to cross the road, you have a heart attack on the way home, aneurysm in your sleep. This is your eternity; it has tremendous urgency. You know, fifteen hundred thousand people die every twenty-four hours… fifteen hundred thousand! We think death is what always happens to other people, but it's going to happen to us, so please have a sense of urgency and examine my motive. Why would I talk to you like this? It's only because I love you. I care about you. I'd hate for you to end up in hell. I'd hate for you to leave here and say, "That was good. That was interesting. I'm going to think about this," and you die in your sins. Say, "God please forgive me." Will you do that?

DAMIAN: Yes, sir.

RAY: Do you have a Bible at home?

DAMIAN: Yes, sir.

RAY: Can I give you something we've published called *The Bible's Four Gospels*? I'd love to give it to you. Is that okay?

DAMIAN: Yes.

RAY: Would you be embarrassed if I pray with you?

DAMIAN: No, of course not.

RAY: Father, I pray for Damian; thank you for his open heart today, for his desire to get right with you. Thank you that he's acknowledged his sins, and please grant repentance to acknowledging the truth, and may he today fling himself upon the Savior and trust in your amazing grace. In Jesus' name we pray, amen.

DAMIAN: Amen.

I felt encouraged. When I first discovered his Mormon background, I wondered if I would have to try to counter unbiblical doctrines. But I didn't have to do that. He was humble and eventually honest about his sins. Sin blinds us from the truth of the gospel. It's not just a mistake but what separates us from the Creator. Recognizing this allows us to turn to Jesus in repentance and accept his mercy.

CHAPTER 16

A CONTRITE HEART

It was April 2022, and I was delighted to finally see students at a local college again after it had been deserted for two years because of the COVID-19 pandemic. Red was standing alone as Sam (my dog) and I rode up to her on my electric bike. As I explained about the YouTube channel and asked her to come on camera, I fought negative thoughts. She seemed very introverted, so I expected the interview would lack color. I was *very* wrong.

RAY: Are you afraid of death?

RED: Somewhat. It is a very interesting topic, I think. The fact that we can't know what happens after death is what makes it scary for a lot of people.

RAY: What do you think you can't know?

RED: Death is the final barrier that you can't come back from when you pass through it.

RAY: Have you ever put together an appliance without reading the instructions and made a mess of it?

RED: Oh yes, definitely. The instruction book is essential for anything.

RAY: The maker knows best, who gives the instructions to make the appliance work. The Bible is God's instruction book.

RED: That makes sense.

RAY: In the Old Testament, God promised to destroy death. The New Testament tells us how he did it. Did you know that?

RED: I did not.

RAY: Have you ever studied the Bible?

RED: No.

It's a little easier for me when someone says that they haven't studied the Bible. This is because it gives me a clean slate to deal with. I don't have to battle someone who has read the Bible and tossed it aside, thinking it irrelevant.

RAY: Let me tell you what the Bible says. The reason you die is because God has given you the death sentence. It says, "The wages of sin is death" [Romans 6:23]. In other words, sin is so serious to God that he is paying you in death for your sins; that's what we have earned. Do you think you are sinful enough for God to be justified to put you to death?

RED: I'd hope not.

RAY: This is the mistake that most people make; they think God is just like us, that he has our moral standard, but the Bible says he is morally perfect. So do you think you are a good person?

RED: I would hope so. I do my best to be a good person.

RAY: So how many lies have you told in your life?

RED: I don't think there is a number that most people would be able to quantify.

RAY: Have you ever stolen something, even if it is small, in your whole life? Irrespective of its value?

RED: Not on purpose.

RAY: Have you ever used God's name in vain?

RED: Yes.

RAY: Do you love your mom?

RED: [Nods]

RAY: Would you use her name as a cuss word?

RED: No.

RAY: You would never do that because that would dishonor her. It would disrespect her, but you have not honored the God who gave you your mother or gave you your life. You have used his name in the place of [a cuss] word, which is called blasphemy. It is very serious in God's eyes, so serious it is punishable by death. So, I am giving you the standard that God's going to judge with on judgment day. Jesus said if you look with lust—do you know what lust is?

RED: [Nods]

RAY: If you look with lust, you commit adultery in your heart. Have you looked with lust?

RED: I don't believe I have.

RAY: Have you ever hated somebody?

RED: I have to say yes.

RAY: The Bible says, "He who hates his brother is a murderer" [1 John 3:15, author's para-phrase]. That is how high God's standards are. Let me give you a quick summation. Red, this isn't me judging you; this is for you to judge yourself. You have told me you are a liar, a blas-phemer, and a murderer at heart. That is how God sees you. So if he judges you by the Ten Commandments, we've looked at five of them, on judgment day, are you going to be innocent or guilty?

It would be a great mistake to take a criminal aside after his guilt has been established and tell him that the judge didn't see his crime as being anything serious. That would dissipate the criminal's contrition. Why should he be sorry for his crime if the judge isn't concerned? Rather, the criminal should be aware of the frown on the face of the judge. The crime is serious, and the criminal's attitude should be sober. God is so serious about Red's sin that he has given her the death sentence, and she needed to know that. Otherwise she would continue to think lightly of sin and, consequently, of the Savior.

RED: God will consider me guilty for that.

RAY: Heaven or hell?

RED: Sounds like hell to me.

RAY: Does that concern you?

RED: I know I should say yes. But if those are God's standards, then so be it.

RAY: It may not concern you, but, Red, it horrifies me. I just met you, but I care about you. I even love you. I hardly even know you, but I want to see you in heaven. The thought of you ending up in hell takes my breath away. It is so terrible. Death is evidence that God is serious about sin. Do you know what God did for guilty sinners so that we wouldn't have to go to hell?

RED: I don't believe I know.

RAY: You probably know, but you don't understand it. Have you heard of Jesus dying on the cross?

RED: I have.

RAY: Okay. It is as simple as this: you and I broke God's law, the Ten Commandments. Jesus paid the fine. Just before he dismissed his spirit, he said, "It is finished" [John 19:30]. That is a strange thing to say when you are dying, but he was saying that the debt has been paid. We broke God's law; Jesus paid the fine.

Red, if you are in court and you have gotten speeding fines, the judge will let you go if someone else pays them. He'll say, "Red, there are a lot of speeding fines, but someone has paid them. You are out of here. You can leave." Even though you are guilty, you can walk because someone paid your fine. And even though you and I are guilty before God of serious crimes, he can let us walk. He can forgive us, legally, because Jesus paid the fine. He evened the scales through his death and resurrection.

And all you have to do to find everlasting life is repent of your sins, that means to be sorry for your sins and to turn from them. Don't play the hypocrite but be genuine in your faith. And then trust in Jesus like you trust a parachute. You are like someone on the edge of a plane ten thousand feet up. They know they have to jump, but they don't have a parachute. It is really scary, but this is their plan: they are going to flap their arms and try to save themselves. You and I would say to that person, "Don't do that. It's not going to work. Just trust the parachute."

So, don't try to save yourself on judgment day by thinking you are a good person because you are not. You are like the rest of us. You are a sinner. Simply transfer your trust from yourself to the Savior, and the minute you do that, you've got God's promise that he will forgive every sin you've ever committed…all those secret sins that nobody knew about but God saw. He will wash them away in an instant—not because you are good but because God is good and kind and rich in mercy. Is this making sense?

RED: It is.

RAY: So, Red, if you were to die today and God gave you justice, you'd be justly damned. There are two things you must do to be saved: you must repent and trust alone in Jesus. When are you going to do that?

RED: I cannot say I have a definite answer. But I am sure it is something I would want to do someday.

RAY: Well, think of it like this. You are on a plane ten thousand feet up. If you jump, you are going to hit the ground at 120 miles an hour. You *have* to jump. I say, "Are you going to put the parachute on?"

You say, "It is something I'm going to consider one day." But the best thing I can do for you would be to hang you out of the plane by your ankles for five seconds, then pull you in, and you will say, "Oh, give me that parachute! This is terrifying."

And what I have tried to do is to hang you at eternity by your ankles just for a few minutes so you get fear in your heart because that fear is your friend, not your enemy. If it makes you put on a parachute, it is doing you a favor. And if it makes you come to Christ and say, "God forgive me; I am a sinner," it is doing you a great favor. The Bible says, "Through the fear of the Lord, men depart from evil" [Proverbs 16:6, author's paraphrase].

And we'll never let go of our sins as long as we think we are good people or we procrastinate, that is, we put things off. So, I want you to think about it with this sense of sobriety. What if you die today…what if you die tonight? One hundred fifty thousand people die every twenty-four hours. So when do you think you'll get right with God? Don't feel pressured by me, but be pressured by common sense. Okay? When do you think you are going to get right with the Lord?

RED: I know the correct answer is right now. But faith is a big thing to a lot of people, and I would need to come to that answer on my own, eventually.

Her "faith is a big thing to a lot of people" caught my attention because it carried negative connotations. If I was speaking about having faith in my wife and someone said that it was a big thing for a lot of people, I would be offended. Faith in my wife isn't a big thing. It's not hard; it's easy. She is trustworthy. Once people understand the trustworthiness of God, faith comes naturally.

RAY: Just let me tell you something about faith. I'll teach you a little lesson about faith that may really help you. Do you live in this area?

RED: I do.

RAY: What are you studying at school?

RED: I'm currently majoring in English.

RAY: I don't believe any of that. I don't believe you are from this area or that you are majoring in English. If I don't have faith in your integrity and you are speaking the truth, it is an insult to you as a human being. And so, don't insult God with a lack of faith. Just say, "I trust the Lord. He gave me life. He gave me my brain. He gave me my eyes. He gave me my ability to breathe, the blueness of the sky, the love of a family." All these things are a gift from God, and so, have faith in him. Trust him with all your heart.

We trust pilots, we trust taxi drivers, we trust doctors, we trust surgeons, and all those people can let us down, but God will never let you down because he has no sin. It is impossible for God to lie, the Bible says, and that is wonderful news for you and me. We can believe everything he says in his Word. So are you going to think about what we talked about?

RED: I will.

RAY: Correct me if I am wrong, but, Red, I noticed a number of times you teared up. You had tears in your eyes. Why is that?

RED: [With tears beginning to fall down her face] I was raised in a Christian family, so, you know, what you said is very familiar.

RAY: There is something happening in your heart, isn't it?

RED: It seems so.

RAY: All I can say is the Bible says genuine sorrow for sin is pleasing to God [see 2 Corinthians 7:9–10]. The Bible says the sacrifices of God are a broken spirit and a contrite heart [see Psalm 51:17]. Do you know what contrition is?

RED: No.

RAY: It means to be sorry for your sins. That is what a judge looks for in a criminal. If the criminal is sorry and he sees a tear in his eye, the judge will give him mercy. So, get before the Lord and say, "God, forgive me. I am a sinner," and he won't despise that. He will greet you with open arms, forgive you, and give you a new heart with new desires. Can I pray for you?

RED: Of course.

RAY: Father, I pray for Red, that this day she will come to you with a good and honest heart and understand not only your justice and your anger against sin but also your love and mercy that you have extended on the cross. This day, please, speak to her heart, transform her. May she be born again, and may she love and serve you, the God who gave her life—for the rest of her life. In Jesus' name we pray, amen. [Hands her the *Million Dollar Gospel of John*] Isn't that cool?

RED: It *is* cool.

RAY: Your family are Christians, is that right?

RED: Yes.

RAY: They have been praying for you, and that is why you have listened today. They love you, and so do we, and so does God. God bless you.

RED: You too.

This interview left a lot of people on our YouTube channel in tears. Multiple people said that they wanted to hug her. Others asked why I hadn't given her a hug. I actually did. But I removed it from the footage because some may have been offended or distracted. I leave most witnessing encounters with a rejoicing heart. But with Red, I wanted to leap over the moon. I'm sure angels rejoiced that day.

In every witnessing encounter, I have one aim. I want to answer the *Why Jesus?* question. I want everyone to see the answer—because there is no other name under heaven given among humans whereby we must be saved. Only he is the way, the truth, and the life. Only he can save us from death.

CONCLUSION

Hindsight is said to be 20/20. In other words, when we look back, we can often see things more clearly. This is particularly true about history. Back in the 1930s, many considered the French army and its tanks some of the best in the world. But when Germany tested the French force in battle, the French were found to be sorely lacking. The German tanks outclassed the French ones, which turned out to be mechanically unreliable gas guzzlers. The powerful German army conquered the French in less than two months. It's easy to be confident when you have a plan, but you can never prepare for every move your opponents will make or every resource they may have.

You and I may have plans to reach the lost, but those plans will fail if we don't have powerful and reliable weapons. This book was written to show you that the weapons God has given us are both mighty and trustworthy. One of our greatest weapons is the law of God. Study how to use it and then be prepared to use it—as Jesus did. The Scriptures speak of "the preparation of the gospel of peace" (Ephesians 6:15). The *Amplified Bible* says of that verse: "having strapped on your feet the gospel of peace in preparation [to face the enemy with firm-footed stability and the readiness produced by the good news]."

Jesus is our example. He shows us how to reach the lost. So never hesitate to use the Ten Commandments to stop a sinner's mouth, to show sinners their danger, to surround them with terrible darkness, and to help them to clearly see Jesus.

We are waiting for a kingdom that cannot be moved so we can be saved from death's claws—humanity's greatest predator. May we be ever grateful for what we have been saved from and for the treasure that we have in Christ: "When Christ who is our life appears, then you also will appear with Him in glory. Therefore put to death your members which are on the earth: fornication, uncleanness, passion, evil desire, and covetousness, which is idolatry. Because of these things the wrath of God is coming upon the sons of disobedience, in which you yourselves once walked when you lived in them" (Colossians 3:4–7).

But don't let your gratitude stop there. Think about the children of disobedience. Think about how sin once deceived you with its pleasures, and then think soberly of this evil world's terrible fate. Such thoughts should put wings in our feet. We should daily pray for and run to the lost and plead with them to repent and trust in Jesus—because their precious lives depend on it.

And every encounter we have with the lost should have its culmination in him. *Why Jesus?* Because there is no other name under heaven whereby we must be saved. *He* is the way, the truth, and the life.

I hope the following emails I have received will encourage you as much as they encouraged me. They are heartening to me because they are fruit from past years, and they can also encourage you because they are a reminder that your faithful laboring now will bear fruit in due season. This one is from a judge in Florida, who joyfully gave permission to use his email although we cannot use his name because of his position:

> Mr. Comfort,
>
> Twenty-seven years ago, in March 1994, you spoke at a Christian school in Dallas, Texas, called Christ for the Nations. You probably thought you were speaking to a crowd of Christian students at the lunch hour, motivating them to share the gospel. But I was also there visiting my sister that week and heard all you had to say about the existence of God (proven by a banana and a can of Coke), repentance (that "sin is exceedingly sinful"), and the saving blood of Jesus. I was an atheist, a product of the public school system's teaching of Darwinism and evolution. I had just been kicked out of my house a

year and a half prior and, frankly, was in a pretty worthless state. God used what you shared to completely redirect the course of my life.

God convicted my heart of his own reality, the depravity of my condition, and my need to trust Christ as my Savior and live for him. But that is not all. I got to see how you lived your life. I can only imagine as a father now, what a sacrifice it must have been for you to spend essentially the entire week on campus, walking through the gym to tell people, "Why are you wasting time on your earthly body when you will get a new one in heaven," (Yep, I was one of the guys you said that to as well) and taking out teams to street evangelize while passing out tracts. It was not only the gospel but your life lived for Christ that had a profound and lasting impact on me. I was eighteen years old at the time, and now I am forty-six. I still remember your testimony, and I attempt to emulate that in my own witnessing life (albeit, I fall short often, but I am on a growth track).

I figured it may encourage you to know that the "seed" you planted and watered way back then has taken root in good soil. I came out of that week at Christ for the Nations saved and with a new vision for my life. I had a desire to serve God, to be in a committed relationship someday, and to use my gifts and talents for his glory. I think about the passage, "Whatever you do to the least of these, you have done it unto me" [Matthew 25:40, author's paraphrase]. I was "the least of these." What you did for me, you really did for Jesus.

Since I saw you in 1994, I have consistently been involved in evangelistic churches. I have traveled on many mission trips, foreign and domestic. I have seen several of my family members come to a saving faith in Christ. God guided me to go to law school, where I met my wife of now almost twenty-four years. We have four amazing children, all of whom we have raised in church. At God's guidance, I also served four years in the military after 9/11. My wife and I are constantly sharing tracts—pretty much yours exclusively. I tell people, "This is written by a man who shared this with me years ago." God has called me to public service as well in the state which I am living. It is one of many platforms the Lord has given me to witness to others.

Mr. Comfort, I hope this email reaches you. I hope it is an encouragement to you. Galatians 6:9 tells us that if we do not grow weary in doing good, we will reap a harvest if we do not lose heart. You have not grown weary in doing good. Your life and witness are reaping a harvest. I hope this encourages you to keep running the race, my precious brother. If I don't get to meet you in person on this side of heaven, I will be the first in line knocking at your door up there!

Look at this person testifying as to how God's law spoke to his heart:

Just want to say I grew up in the South, so at a very young age, I knew who Jesus was and what he did on the cross for us. It wasn't until last year when I first started watching Living Waters YouTube channel that I put it all together. I was born again because of the law speaking to my heart. Ever since then, the Holy Spirit has filled me up and done amazing things in my life. I've been the youth director at my church now about five months, and I can't stop watching these videos and diving deep in the Word. Thank y'all for preaching the law before the gospel because I would still be lost in this world without hearing it.

There are many signs of the end of age that come to mind when it comes to biblical prophecy: the Jews obtaining Jerusalem, the coming battle of Armageddon, wars, nation rising against nation, plagues, rebellious youth, increased lawlessness, skeptics, mockers of God, a lukewarm church, hearts failing for fear of things coming on the earth, and many others.

However, there is one sign of the last days that is hardly ever mentioned. Jesus spoke of it after giving a long list of end-times signs. It is almost the climax of his discourse: "And this gospel of the kingdom shall be preached in all the world for a witness unto all nations; and then shall the end come" (Matthew 24:14 KJV).

The proclamation of the gospel is a major end-times sign. Notice the word *shall*. The gospel "shall be preached." There is no holding it back. Just think of it—*every time you share the gospel with an unsaved person, God is using you to fulfill Bible prophecy*. And if you are doing that, you are not only being wonderfully used by God, but you are also in one sense hastening the second coming of Jesus Christ.

Let me ask you a question based on something Jesus said to his disciples. He said, "The harvest truly is great, but the laborers are few; therefore pray the Lord of the harvest to send out laborers into His harvest" (Luke 10:2).

Are you doing that? Are you praying that God will raise up laborers? We need to regularly and earnestly pray for that because laborers are still comparably few in number. Reaching the lost isn't the number one priority of most of the contemporary church. But it certainly should be. So let's not only pray that God raises up laborers, but let's then put legs to our prayers and take this glorious gospel to this lost and dying world. "How beautiful are the feet of those who preach the gospel of peace, who bring glad tidings of good things!" (Romans 10:15).

ENDNOTES

1   Mary Bowerman, "8-Year-Old Learns to Drive on YouTube, Heads to McDonald's," *USA Today*, last updated April 13, 2017, https://www.usatoday.com/story/news/nation-now/2017/04/13/8-year-old-learns-drive-youtube-heads-mcdonalds/100408432/.

2   Charles Haddon Spurgeon, "Coming Judgement of the Secrets of Man," The Spurgeon Center for Biblical Preaching at Midwestern Seminary, sermon given July 12, 1885, accessed June 9, 2022, https://www.spurgeon.org/resource-library/sermons/coming-judgement-of-the-secrets-of-man/#flipbook/.

3   "George Harrison Dies at 58," *Billboard*, November 30, 2001, https://www.billboard.com/music/music-news/george-harrison-dies-at-58-77597/.

4   Emerson Fittipaldi, "A Spiritual Conversation with Emerson Fittipaldi," interview by Felipe Assis, May 26, 2019, produced by Crossbridge Church | Key Biscayne, YouTube video, 30:14, https://www.youtube.com/watch?v=m-WUwqLb4d0.

5   You can read *God Has a Wonderful Plan for Your Life* for free on FreeWonderfulBook.com.

6   Ray Comfort, *God Has a Wonderful Plan for Your Life: The Myth of the Modern Message* (Bellflower, CA: Living Waters Publications, 2010), 21–22.

7   J. Gordon Melton, "Wicca," *Encyclopedia Britannica*
     (website), last updated February 2, 2021, https://www.
     britannica.com/topic/Wicca.

8   "What Are Familiar Spirits?," Got Questions, accessed
     July 22, 2022, https://www.gotquestions.org/familiar-
     spirits.html.

9   "What Are Familiar Spirits?"

10   "What Are the Gnostic Gospels?," Got Questions,
     accessed July 22, 2022, https://www.gotquestions.org/
     Gnostic-gospels.html.

11   "*The Batman*," Movieguide, accessed May 25, 2022,
     https://www.movieguide.org/reviews/the-batman.html.

12   "*The Batman*."

13   "How Does YouTube Manage Harmful Content?,"
     YouTube, accessed May 25, 2022, https://www.
     youtube.com/howyoutubeworks/our-commitments/
     managing-harmful-content/.

14   Charles Phillips and Alan Axelrod, eds., *Encyclopedia
     of Wars*, vol. 3 (New York: Facts on File, 2005),
     1484–85.

15   A. W. Tozer, *The Knowledge of the Holy*, in *Three
     Spiritual Classics in One Volume* (Chicago: Moody
     Publishers, 2018), 152.

16   Bruce R. McConkie, *Mormon Doctrine* (Salt Lake
     City, UT: Deseret Book Company, 1966), 472,
     PDF, https://ia800500.us.archive.org/35/items/
     MormonDoctrine1966/MormonDoctrine1966.pdf.

17 Andrew Skinner et al., "Introduction and
    Historic Overview" (discussion), March 7,
    2004, produced by BYU Religious Education,
    YouTube video, 28:06, https://www.youtube.com/
    watch?v=50RIZCqnXq0&list=PLc5yYrpPFm
    2u8cgwhncfMrfnCgsSWOGaK.

ABOUT THE AUTHOR

Ray Comfort is the best-selling author of more than one hundred books. He is the cohost of an award-winning television program that airs in 190 countries and the producer of award-winning movies that have been viewed by millions (see www.FullyFreeFilms.com). He lives in Southern California with his wife, Sue, and has three grown children. For more information, visit LivingWaters.com.